Mozart's BRAIN

AND THE

FIGHTER PILOT

Mozart's BRAIN

AND THE

RICHARD RESTAK, M.D.

THREE RIVERS PRESS
NEW YORK

FIGHTER PILOT

PILOT ∾

UNLEASHING

YOUR BRAIN'S

POTENTIAL

Published by Three Rivers Press, New York, New York.
Member of the Crown Publishing Group, a division of Random House, Inc.

www.randomhouse.com

Three Rivers Press is a registered trademark and the Three Rivers Press colophon is a trademark of Random House, Inc.

Originally published in hardcover by Harmony Books, a division of Random House, Inc., in 2001.

Printed in the United States of America

DESIGN BY ELINA D. NUDELMAN

ILLUSTRATION CREDITS
All chapter-opening illustrations by Susan Hunt Yule

Page 22—Alan Witschonke

Pages 23 and 192—Dale Purves et al., *Neuroscience 1/e,* copyright © 1997 by Sinauer Associates, Inc. Reprinted with permission from Sinauer Associates, Inc.

Page 39—*Neurology Reviews.* 2000; 8(6):57. Reprinted with permission from *Neurology Reviews.*

Page 48—Richard M. Restak, M.D., *Brainscapes,* copyright © 1995 by Richard M. Restak, M.D. Reprinted with permission from Hyperion.

Grateful acknowledgment is made to **Houghton Mifflin Company** for permission to reprint an illustration from *Brain Power* by Vernon H. Mark, F.A.C.S., with Jeffrey P. Mark, M.Sc. Copyright © 1989 by Vernon H. Mark and Jeffrey Paul Mark. All rights reserved. Reprinted by permission of Houghton Mifflin Company.

Library of Congress Cataloging-in-Publication Data
Restak, Richard M., 1942–
   Mozart's brain and the fighter pilot : unleashing your brain's potential / by Richard Restak.—1st ed.
    1. Brain—Popular works.   2. Mental health—Popular works.   3. Cognition—Popular works.   I. Title.
   QP376 .R4728 2001
   612.8'2—dc21   2001024779

ISBN 0-609-81005-7

10 9 8 7 6 5 4 3 2

First Paperback Edition

To my sister, Louise

Contents

Mozart's BRAIN

AND THE

FIGHTER PILOT

Introduction

*M*ost of us would like to be smarter. But how do we go about improving our mental prowess? That question isn't easily answered. For one thing, even if we could somehow raise our IQ a few points (as promised by many books and programs currently on the market), such an achievement wouldn't necessarily imply that intellectually we'd really be any better off. We all know people with high IQs whose adult accomplishments are less than impressive. A more realistic goal is to enhance our mental functioning in certain key areas that psychologists refer to as cognition.

Briefly, cognition refers to the ability of our brain to attend, identify, and act. More informally, cognition refers to our thoughts, moods, inclinations, decisions, and actions. Included among the components of cognition are alertness, concentration, perceptual speed, learning, memory, problem solving, creativity, and mental endurance. Each of these components of cognition has two things in common. First, each is dependent on how well our brain is functioning. Second, each can be improved by our own efforts. In short, we can make ourselves smarter by enhancing the components of cognition. This book will provide you with methods for enhancing cognition by improving your brain's performance.

Regular exercise of your brain's cognitive powers is the first step. Most of us now incorporate into our daily life some form of regular physical exercise. We do this because such efforts improve our general physical health and, in addition, make us feel better. A similar situation exists when it comes to exercising our brain. The more we exercise it, the better it performs and the better we feel. In addition, the brain, in contrast to other physical organs, doesn't wear out with repeated and sustained use. On the contrary, the brain improves the more we challenge it. This observation has led to a fundamental principle about the brain's operation: use it or lose it.

Think back to a talent or skill that you developed by practice and application but subsequently allowed to languish. Perhaps you were a decent piano player at one time in your life, but later stopped your lessons because you didn't "have the time to practice." Or maybe— like me—you took chess lessons that enabled you to become a moderately competitive player. Competitive, that is, until you dismissed your instructor, canceled the chess magazine subscriptions, and gradually gave up the game.

In both of these instances—music and chess—changes took place in your brain. After the initial establishment of circuits for music and chess, your brain underwent a kind of atrophy as the circuits important for these activities disappeared secondary to disuse.

Fortunately, the brain is highly resilient and has a lifetime memory. Those music and chess circuits can be revived. All that's required is that you once again start playing the piano (or some other instrument), or take up your chess lessons and engage in regular chess matches with some challenging players. This is possible because throughout our lives the brain retains a high degree of plasticity; it changes in response to experience. If the experiences are rich and varied, the brain will develop a greater number of nerve cell connections. If the experiences are dull and infrequent, the connections will either never form or die off. We know this from studies carried out on laboratory animals.

If an animal is provided with a stimulating, challenging environment like a cage filled with toys, that animal's brain will show a dramatic increase in the number of nerve cell connections. The animal's brain will be heavier with larger nerve cells in some areas than in animals that are reared in barren, comparatively deprived laboratory cages. This increase in brain weight results from an increase in the number of synapses—electrochemical connections—between neurons.

As mentioned, a similar process occurs in the human brain. You can preselect the kind of brain you will have by choosing richly varied experiences. The process starts in childhood and continues until the day you die. Incidentally, this insight—that the brain retains its plasticity across the entire life span—is a comparatively recent one. When I wrote my first book on the human brain in 1979, I didn't hear much from the scientists I interviewed about the plasticity of the mature, adult brain. At that time, most people—scientists included—believed that as the brain matured and formed its nerve cell connections, those connections stayed in place until finally dropping out in old age. Few people thought of the brain as being susceptible to change in its actual structure.

Now, thanks to research like the experiments mentioned above, we know that the brain is much more malleable and subject to change. Indeed, we have no choice about whether or not our brain will change from the way it is today. The real question is: Will we help bring about positive, enriching changes in our brain's structure and function, or will we allow it to undergo "disuse atrophy"?

It's important to remember that our brain holds the key to everything we will ever accomplish. Indeed, the brain is the gateway for all of our sensations and the weaver of all of our experiences. And while most of us are convinced that exercise increases our physical well-being, it's less commonly appreciated that the brain also must be exercised; it's a dynamic structure that improves with use and challenge. I became convinced of this while researching two previous books on longevity. Simply put, an otherwise healthy older person can reduce his or her risk for developing dementia (formerly referred to as senility) by remaining mentally active. But the benefits of an active, challenged brain aren't limited to late in life. Rather, the "use it or lose it" formula applies to each of us no matter what our age.

Moreover, the healthy exercise of our brain's inherent powers is highly pleasurable. Think back to occasions when you scored well on a test or prevailed in a debate or found yourself unable to put down a certain book because of the excitement you experienced while reading it. Your pleasure in each of these instances came from the exercise of your brain's cognitive powers. Further, there are specific steps you can take to increase and strengthen these powers. In essence, you can achieve more of the things that you desire by enhancing your brain's cognitive functioning.

For instance, memory is probably the most important cognitive function. We are what we remember. If you doubt this, spend a few minutes with people suffering from Alzheimer's disease. They no longer remember the most important and noteworthy events in their lives. Not only do they not remember their marriages, but they may no longer even recognize their spouses. Ask them what they once did for a living and your answer may consist of nothing more than a blank stare.

Contrast this to a person endowed with a rich memory, who can recall events and people with clarity and richness. Thanks to memory, he or she can respond to detailed questions about the past and link that past with the present. The ability to recall conversations, family vacations, favorite movies and books, appointments, and social engagements depends on memory.

Yet we also recognize that poor memories aren't limited to those who suffer from Alzheimer's and other diseases. Some of us are lucky and can remember faces and names from the distant past. Those of us with natural memory gifts have only to be told something once in order to have it readily available for instant recall. Fortunately, for those endowed with a less-efficient memory, steps can be taken to improve it.

Useful and effective memory systems can be traced back as far as the Greeks. Aristotle wrote a short book on memory and compared the mind to a wax tablet that received the impressions of all new information. He suggested that with the passage of time the clarity of the wax image would fade unless steps were taken to preserve it. Plato possessed prodigious powers of recall and considered memory as a force for personal integration with the spiritual forces of the cosmos. Metrodorus, a first-century B.C. Greek writer, astounded friends and colleagues with his ability to remember conversations he had had with them sometimes years earlier. Indeed, the Greeks so venerated memory that they transformed it into a goddess—Mnemosyne, mother of the Muses.

But the greatest contribution of the Greeks to our contemporary understanding of memory was the insistence, starting with Plato, that memory could be trained. They originated the liberating idea that we don't simply have to accept our natural memory talents or lack thereof. It is possible for us to improve our memory. The same can be said about all of the other components of cognition.

This book will provide you with specific positive steps you can take to get smarter and stay smarter. It is based on an important principle: The more you learn about how your brain works, the better your chances of using it most efficiently, optimizing your intellectual capabilities, and accomplishing even more in life than many people who may score higher than you on standardized intelligence tests.

What follows are twenty-eight suggestions and some accompanying exercises for enhancing your brain's performance. These suggestions are based on my own experiences over a career that has included the writing of twelve books on the human brain while simultaneously maintaining a full-time practice in neurology and neuropsychiatry. In response to the competing demands of this dual-career track, I learned how to get the best possible performance from my brain. After discovering what worked for me, I started several years ago compiling a list of suggestions anyone can follow in order to increase his or her brain efficiency.

My aim in *Mozart's Brain and the Fighter Pilot* is to convey to you an understanding of the basic principles of brain operation. Once you understand those principles, you can follow the twenty-eight suggestions and perhaps even come up with some more of your own based on sound operating principles that will help you improve your brain function. Let's start right off with the first, and in many ways the most important, of the suggestions outlined in this book.

1

Learn as much as possible about how your brain works.

This is the most important factor in getting smart and staying smart. In order to do this, you don't have to become a neurologist or subscribe to scholarly journals on neuroscience (the study of the brain at every operating level ranging from everyday observable behavior to brain processes taking place at the level of chemicals and molecules). Here is a useful summary of the facts you should know.

The adult human brain weighs about three pounds and consists of about 100 billion nerve cells or neurons along with an even greater number of non-neuronal cells called glia (in Greek, *glia* means "glue") interspersed among the neurons. The neurons are responsible for the communication of information throughout the brain. Especially important is the brain's outer wrinkled mantle, the cerebral cortex, which gives the brain the appearance of a gnarled walnut. The cerebral cortex contains about 30 billion neurons linked to one another by means of a million billion neuronal connections called synapses.

As pointed out by Nobel Prize–winning neuroscientist Gerald Edelman, more than 32 million years would be required to count all of the synapses in the human brain at a counting rate of one synapse per second. And if we concentrate on the number of possible neuronal connections (circuits) within the brain, we get an even more astounding number: 10 followed by a million zeros. To put that number into some kind of perspective, consider that the number of particles in the known universe comes to only 10 followed by seventy-nine zeros. Finally, consider that the glia, which exceed the number of neurons by at least a power of 10, are also believed to be capable of communication. If this is true, then the number of possible brain states exceeds even our most extravagant projections.

Any of the brain's 100 or so billion neurons can potentially communicate with any other via one or more linkages. Indeed, each neuron is no more than two or three degrees of separation from another. Linkages, once formed, are strengthened by repetition. At the behavioral level, this takes the form of habit. Each time you practice a piano piece or a golf swing (presuming you are doing it correctly), your performance improves. This corresponds at the neuronal level to the establishment and facilitation of neuronal circuits.

The cerebral cortex consists of the outer gray matter of the cerebral hemispheres and the cerebellum, the two structures that contain most of the neurons in the brain. Less than a quarter inch in thickness, this thin rind (*cortex* in the original Latin means "rind"), includes some 85 percent of all brain tissue. An obvious feature of the cerebral cortex is its highly convoluted surface and wrinkled appearance. This wrinkling serves the purpose of increasing the surface area of this thin outer layer without a corresponding increase in volume and size (similar to wrinkling a handkerchief so that the larger surface area can be contained in the smaller confines of a wallet or small purse).

While it's true that certain brain areas are specialized (such as the centers for processing sight, sound, touch, and other qualities and properties), the largest portion of the brain, the association cortex, is devoted to establishing networks and thereby linking everything together throughout the brain. As a result of this networking, you don't separately see, hear, taste, smell, and feel your breakfast bagel—you experience it as a unity. It's the association cortex that makes that possible. Figure B, on page 23, shows the association cortex. Notice that it makes up more than 90 percent of the brain. Figure A, on page 22, depicts the other major brain areas along with some of their specialized functions. Notice that the right and left hemispheres are specialized for different functions as depicted in Figure C, on page 24, and discussed in detail later in the book.

Below the cerebral hemispheres lies a group of nuclei (collections of nerve cells) that organize movement. These nuclei, called the basal ganglia, enable you to do such things as skillfully maneuver your way through heavy traffic while simultaneously rehearsing what you're going to say at the business meeting later in the morning. In computer terms, the cerebral cortex writes the software programs for actions and, after some practice on your part, the basal ganglia take over to run the programs that enable you to carry out the actions. When you learn the tango, for instance, you have to concentrate (i.e., use the cerebral cortex) to plan, learn, and get comfortable with the steps. But after some practice and experience, you're eventually able to tango while thinking of other things because the basal ganglia are operating that system automatically.

Toward the back of the brain resides the cerebellum, a center involved in movement, balance, and coordination. The last time you watched a gymnast at the top of his or her form you were watching the cerebellum operating at its highest level. But the structure is not just for balance and coordination; it is also involved in the planning activities that precede movement.

Nevertheless, as we will illustrate throughout this book, the brain can't be considered only in terms of its separate components. Think of it as a unified structure in which each part contributes toward its total functioning. As an example, suppose you suddenly decide you'd like a pizza. That thought is formulated as an action plan by the frontal lobes, which are located just behind your forehead, and results in impulses directed to the cerebellum. Your cerebellum, along with

Figure A

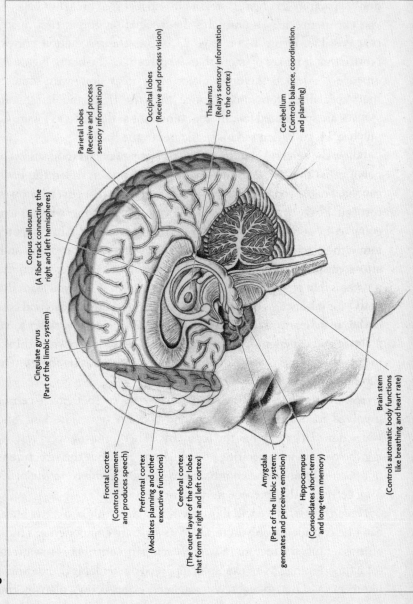

Cingulate gyrus
(Part of the limbic system)

Corpus callosum
(A fiber track connecting the
right and left hemispheres)

Parietal lobes
(Receive and process
sensory information)

Occipital lobes
(Receive and process vision)

Thalamus
(Relays sensory information
to the cortex)

Cerebellum
(Controls balance, coordination,
and planning)

Frontal cortex
(Controls movement
and produces speech)

Prefrontal cortex
(Mediates planning and other
executive functions)

Cerebral cortex
(The outer layer of the four lobes
that form the right and left cortex)

Amygdala
(Part of the limbic system;
generates and perceives emotion)

Hippocampus
(Consolidates short-term
and long-term memory)

Brain stem
(Controls automatic body functions
like breathing and heart rate)

structures from the basal ganglia (sometimes referred to as subcortical motor centers), translates the frontal lobes' action plan into a motor program. First you make a phone call and arrange for the pizza delivery; then you pay the delivery person upon arrival; finally, you sit down, open the box, and reach in for that first slice. Each of these separate motions involves different muscles activated in a different sequence. Or you might use different muscles depending on the circumstances. For instance, if your right elbow is slightly sore from too much tennis, you'll have to eat the pizza with your nondominant left hand. In order to make this switch, your cerebellum formulates a change in the motor program received from the frontal lobes. Indeed, the cerebellum springs into action prior to any perceptible movement on your part. Thus, when your hand approaches the pizza the cerebellum has already predicted and anticipated all of the necessary fine hand and finger movements that will take place over the next minute or so. Such an anticipatory function operates over your entire life span, during which your cerebellum regularly programs hundreds of thousands of action sequences involving every muscle in the body.

But your cerebellum isn't just a glorified personal trainer that integrates muscles into motor programs. The cerebellum is also integral to activities not involving movement at all, such as when you try to solve a problem, or remember someone's name, or maybe just do

Figure B

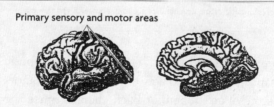

Primary sensory and motor areas

Figure B An outer and inner view of the brain showing the extent of the association cortices. Notice that the primary sensory and motor areas occupy only a small fraction of the total cortical area. The remainder comprises the association cortices and mediates human cognitive processes. The term *association* refers to the fact that these regions of the cortex integrate (associate) information gathered by the other brain regions.

Figure C

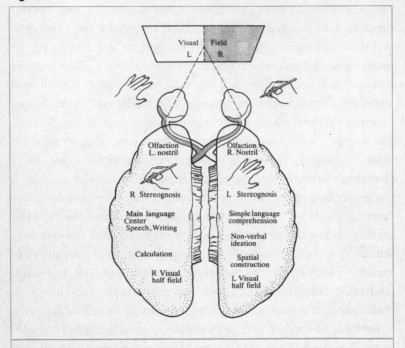

Figure C A schematic summary of the functional arrangement of the right and left hemispheres after surgical resection of the connecting corpus callosum. The impulses from each hand and from the left and right halves of each retina terminate in the opposite hemisphere. In the normal brain this information is collated via transfer across the corpus callosum. But with the corpus callosum cut ("split-brain"), each hemisphere operates in isolation from the other and the processed information from each hemisphere is no longer available to the other. As a result, the exchange of information from one hemisphere to the other fails to take place.

nothing more than sit and think. The cerebellum of music conductors, for instance, springs into action when the conductors listen to or read the score of an unfamiliar Bach chorale. Since the conductors are not moving at the time, their cerebellar activity must relate to their listening to and thinking about the music. As a practical application of this research finding that simply listening to or reading a musical score is sufficient for cerebellar activation, consider boosting your own brain circuitry by refining your musical appreciation and knowledge. As Gordon Shaw, a physicist at the University of California at Irvine, puts it, "music is tapping into an inherent structure of the brain." We'll say more about that "tapping" in chapter 23.

But the findings of cerebellar enhancement are not limited to music. Neuroscientists have known for years that any skilled activity enhances the cerebellum. In addition, we now know that imaging or mentally concentrating on the activities can accomplish a similar result. Of course, that doesn't mean you can become a musician or an athlete by thought alone. You have to undertake the discipline of learning how to play the violin or perfecting your tennis backhand. But once you've made progress in your training, imaging can help activate and sustain the necessary circuits. Extensive two-way connections between cerebellum and frontal cortex make this possible.

Indeed, thought and movement are integrated via the two-directional interplay between the cerebrum—the enlarged wrinkled structure at the top of the brain—and the cerebellum. Mental agility and physical agility complement rather than act in opposition to each other. Therefore, relegate to the Museum of Outmoded Ideas your stereotypes of "dumb" athletes and physically inactive super-power intellects. In most instances, your typical professional athlete spends many hours mentally rehearsing the moves or plays that bring victory. And most writers and other intellectuals try to put aside some time each day for exercise: they've learned that even a short exercise break clears the head and gets the intellectual juices flowing again.

And what about the emotional response to such experiences? That's when the limbic system kicks into gear. The limbic system is a shorthand term for the brain structures within and below the cerebrum. Its most important components are the cingulate gyrus in the cerebrum and the hippocampus and amygdala buried below the cerebral hemispheres.

On the microscopic level, neurons interconnect with one another for the purpose of processing electrical and chemical information. One of the great mysteries of the human brain concerns how these electrical and chemical codes are converted into your desire for that pizza. So far, no one has the solution to the mystery—which is usually referred to as the mind-brain problem. Perhaps nobody will ever solve it, since comparing electrical and chemical events to everyday human decisions is like comparing apples to oranges. When you ordered the pizza, all kinds of interesting activities were going on within your brain—the biological structure one neuroscientist once compared to "an enchanted loom." But how to relate those electrical and chemical changes that take place when you crave a pizza? Nobody has a clue.

Many highly branched processes referred to as dendrites (from the Greek word for "tree") convey incoming information from one neuron to another. (*Arborization* is the term used to convey the treelike appearance and structure of those neurons and their connections. When nerve tissue is looked at through a microscope, the overlapping of the processes of the many neurons looks like the branches of trees.) Each neuron receives information from as many as one thousand other neurons by way of contact on one of its dendrites. The mechanism for transporting outgoing information to another cell involves the axon, a single process that extends outward for varying lengths until reaching its end point, the nerve terminal. By convention, two communicating neurons are referred to as presynaptic (the message carrier) and postsynaptic (the message receiver), with any two communicating cells separated from each other by a tiny space, the synapse.

At the synapse, communication changes from an electrical impulse to a chemical one. Neurotransmitters (chemical messengers) are released from the messenger cell and diffuse across the synapse to lock onto a specialized receptor. Advances over the past three decades in our knowledge about the brain's microscopic and chemical organization have made possible successful treatments for psychiatric illnesses like depression and anxiety. The drugs work by altering the balance of neurotransmitters within the synapse. But the same alteration can be brought about by changes in attitude and behavior. We will say more about this in later chapters.

2

Apply your knowledge about the human brain to organize your ideas.

The preceding Cook's tour of the brain highlights an important principle: the brain is highly interconnected at every level. In fact, you should think of the brain as a vast network wherein every neuron is potentially connectable with every other. And this organization is highly appropriate when you consider the nature of knowledge. Writer and television producer James Burke describes knowledge as "a gigantic and ever-growing sphere in space and time, made up of millions of interconnecting, crisscrossing pathways."

Burke's description of the web of knowledge exactly corresponds to how knowledge is organized within the brain. Everything that we learn is stored in the brain within that vast, interlinking network. And everything within that network is potentially connected to everything else. An important consequence follows from this symmetry.

If you stop learning, and that includes any subject that interests you, your overall mental capacity and performance will decline. That's because of the weakening and eventual loss of brain networks. Such brain alterations don't take place overnight, of course. But over a varying period of time, depending on your previous training and natural abilities, you'll notice a gradual but steady decrease in your powers if you don't nourish and enhance these networks.

For instance, I recently attended a tai chi session. Twenty years ago I had practiced this graceful, slow-motion martial exercise on a daily basis, but I discontinued it about ten years ago after a back injury. Based on my earlier experience with tai chi, I confidently joined the group performing the ancient Chinese exercise in a park near my summer home. I soon discovered to my embarrassment that over the past two decades I had forgotten many of the moves. In essence, the neuronal networks responsible for coding tai chi seemed to have disappeared. (Actually, they haven't disappeared entirely, but have undergone disuse atrophy. If I restart these exercises I can probably reestablish the networks.)

Networking is a fundamental operating principle of the human brain. All knowledge within the brain is based on networking. Thus, any one piece of information can be potentially linked with any other. Indeed, creativity can be thought of as the formation of novel and original linkages. James Burke refers to this as the pinball effect. Rather than training ourselves in narrow specialties, suggests Burke, we should train ourselves "to think in a different way about knowledge and how it should be used."

Philosophers like Aristotle and Thomas Aquinas observed centuries ago that knowledge is a unity with everything potentially connectable with everything else. The World Wide Web is the most conspicuous example in our lifetime of this potential for infinite connection. In his book *Weaving the Web: The Original Design and Ultimate Destiny of the World Wide Web*, Tim Berners-Lee, the inventor of the World Wide Web, emphasizes the importance of the brain in the forming of connections (the italics are mine):

A piece of information is really defined only by what it's related to, and how it's related. There really is little else to meaning. The struc-

ture is everything. There are billions of neurons in our brains, but what are neurons? Just cells. *The brain has no knowledge until connections are made between neurons. All that we know, all that we are, comes from the way our neurons are connected.*

Berners-Lee and Burke both emphasize the brain's vast capacity to form interconnections similar to the vast web of interconnections comprising the World Wide Web. Therefore, think of your brain as a vast assemblage of neurons capable of an infinite number of associations. As you learn new things, increasing linkages become possible. Your ability to comprehend and utilize these linkages is limited only by your powers of memory. Thus, knowledge and, especially, intelligence take on new meanings.

"We might even consider changing our definition of intelligence," suggests Burke. "Instead of judging people by their ability to memorize, to think sequentially and to write good prose, we might measure intelligence by the ability to pinball around through knowledge and make imaginative patterns on the web."

Novelist Hermann Hesse anticipated this new definition of intelligence in his Nobel Prize–winning novel, *Magister Ludi: The Glass Bead Game*. In *Magister Ludi*, ideas held in the mind rather than pieces played on a board form the basis for the game:

The Glass Bead Game is a mode of playing with the total contents and values of our culture. All the insights, noble thoughts and works of art that the human race has produced in its creative eras, all that subsequent periods of scholarly study have reduced to concept and converted into intellectual values, the Glass Bead Game player plays like the organist on an organ. And this organ has attained an almost unimaginable perfection; its manuals and pedals range over the entire intellectual cosmos; its stops are almost without number.

One method of play involves conceptualizing the thoughts and intellectual interactions of thinkers of the past and present. For instance, while playing the Glass Bead Game the player might relate the ideas of these thinkers to each other in the form of analogies, highlighting the similarities and differences among them. A contemporary example of this approach to knowledge is the series Great Books of the Western World.

The late Mortimer Adler, associate editor of the original selection of Great Books, compared the experience of reading them to engaging in a "great conversation." He invoked a picture of

> authors sitting around a table in the same room—totally oblivious to the circumstances of their own time, place and diversity of tongues—confronting each other in agreement, disagreement or otherwise differing about what they have to say on the subject. The sessions of the conference thus imagined would take many days, months, perhaps even years, for it would cover the whole range of ideas and issues that are the objects and concerns of human understanding, always and everywhere.

Readers invited to this "conversation" incorporate the author's ideas and, after some reflection, produce ideas of their own that further refine and expand the knowledge base.

Adler and Hesse touched on a basic insight about knowledge and intelligence: the existence of certain patterns, which underlie the diversity of the world around us and include our own thoughts, feelings, and behaviors. Intelligence enhancement therefore involves creating as many neuronal linkages as possible. But in order to do this we have to extricate ourselves from the confining and limiting idea that knowledge can be broken down into separate "disciplines" that bear little relation to one another.

Instead, according to contemporary game theorist Charles Cameron, "the entire range of ideas can legitimately be brought into play: and this means not only that ideas from different disciplines can be juxtaposed, but also that ideas expressed in 'languages' as diverse as music, painting, sculpture, dance, mathematics and philosophy can be juxtaposed, without first being 'translated' into a common language."

The ideas expressed by Cameron, Hesse, and Adler on intelligence and knowledge can be traced at least as far back as the Renaissance. Indeed, we describe a person possessing varied and far-ranging knowledge as a "Renaissance" person. That is the model we should all strive to achieve. Today we know that the brain is naturally organized to attain those synthetic overviews that draw on knowledge and information from the widest possible sources. In short, our knowledge of the world and our brain share a common structure: a network of nodal points that can potentially be incorporated into an infinity of possible relationships.

3

Think of the brain as the creator of incredibly rich and fascinating montages.

A s a holiday present, my brother Christopher made for me a calendar displaying a montage of events from my life. The month of January, for instance, shows a picture taken of me at about twelve years old, standing with my father and grandfather on the Boardwalk in Atlantic City. To the right of that picture is another taken twenty-five years later on the occasion of my sister's wedding; and beside that is a photo of my sister and me sitting together on a sofa when she was six and I was ten. When seen in juxtaposition, such pictures from widely separated periods of my life achieve a kind of synthesis that defies the seeming logic of chronology. In the present moment, I reprocess those images at the same time: the picture in Atlantic City, my sister's wedding, and she and I as young children sitting together on the sofa.

As another example of my point, my wife and I recently sorted through pictures of our daughter Ann taken at various stages of her life. We were doing this in order to provide suitable pictures for inclusion in her college yearbook. Following my brother's design for the calendar, we chose to create a montage. As we stared at pictures taken from during her infancy to during last month's holiday season, Ann existed simultaneously for us as the senior at Trinity College in Hartford and as the three-year-old in play school. While Ann may have been more comfortable arranging each of these events in their chronological order, since that is how she experienced them, my wife and I could take a different approach. We remember events from every period of Ann's life, starting from her birth and extending to the phone conversation we had with her only a few hours ago. For us, each event from Ann's life seems equally real and contemporary.

Montage is the modus operandi of the brain. Within that three-pound structure, events exist in a nonlinear, nonchronological pattern. Indeed, when I first learned about the brain and its vast network of connections, nodes, and interactions, I began to conceptualize how everything in our lives also forms a seamless unity. In short, by learning about the brain we learn about our experience of the world around us.

Unfortunately, we're taught from earliest childhood to neatly compartmentalize every aspect of our lives into neat parcels like the countries we draw or peruse on our geography maps. It's all too easy to forget that the dividing lines on maps separating those countries are artificial creations based on politics and history. Despite the demarcations and differing colors depicted on the map, the terrain is a seamless unity wherein all of the separate countries blend into one another. The map is not the territory. Nevertheless, it takes a lot of effort to drop all of the artificial barriers about reality that exist only within the confines of our own stilted imaginations.

For instance, time exists as a unity with past, present, and future flowing into one another like one of those montages mentioned a moment ago. Not only can the past influence the present and future, but the future—which by definition doesn't even exist yet—can exert a powerful effect on the present. As an example, the future prospect of an early death or disability resulting as a consequence of your current inactivity can spur you into taking active steps today toward improving your chances of living a longer and more healthy life tomorrow—perhaps by finally joining that hiking club you've heard about.

So, if you want your brain to function optimally, eliminate the tendency to deal with everything in strictly chronological terms. Allow events from different times of your life to coexist in your memory. As philosopher Immanuel Kant and others have suggested, time, space, and chronology are essentially only creations of our brain. Therefore, it's important that you do away with the idea that the world must correspond to illusions of sequence and rational order.

Most of all, remain alert to the occurrence of coincidence. Appreciate coincidence not as the revelation of some deep inner meaning (although that may be true), but as something that can enrich the present moment. For instance, a friend recently attended an antiquarian book fair in order to distract herself momentarily from grief at the loss of her husband. While there, she spent a few moments paging through a rare edition of Timothy Leary's book *The Psychedelic Experience* that she had, as she put it, "just happened to come upon." The book had been one of her husband's favorites. The next day, while speaking on the phone with a friend in Laguna Beach, California, she learned he was buying the former home of a famous writer and thinker. Would she like to guess the writer's identity? She answered without hesitation, "Timothy Leary, of course." At that moment, she vividly experienced a sense of unity: the previous day at the book fair and her unexpected encounter with the Leary book; her grief; and, most important to her, the thought that such a coincidence indicated that her husband was still very much a part of her life. It was as if she and he would remain in contact forever.

When my friend related her book-fair experience I recalled that James Joyce described walking into a library in search of inspiration and aimlessly wandering around, fully expecting to encounter by chance a book relevant to the subject he was thinking of writing about at the time. He expressed a basic trust in this seemingly chaotic method. I think it perfectly complemented his intensely methodical and detailed approach to writing. Of course, the explanation for the method's success is open to several interpretations. Was Joyce (and my friend as well) directed to the relevant books by some unseen force? I guess that's possible, but such an "explanation" is nothing more than an unverifiable, rather eerie act of faith in some unknown mysterious power. In the Joyce example, I prefer a simpler explanation: Joyce incorporated and transformed *whatever* he encountered into literature.

Joyce's method of trusting the present moment to provide him something important for future creativity sounds similar to the method described by Ray Bradbury: "In my early twenties I floundered into a word-association process in which I simply got out of bed each morning, and walked to my desk, and put down any word or series of words that happened along in my head." Mr. Bradbury would then "take arms against the word, or for it, and bring on an assortment of characters to weigh the word and show me its meaning in my own life." Within an hour or two, he would find to his surprise that a new story would be completed.

Bradbury's method takes advantage of the fact that information is stored in the brain via associative links. Think back for a moment to some important event in your life, such as a graduation or a marriage. Your memory for that event doesn't exist in your brain like a video waiting to be placed in a VCR. Instead, the memory changes each time you think about it. At first the changes are subtle, but with succeeding years the changes become more drastic until many years later you have far fewer specific memories of the event. Neuroscientists refer to this process whereby memories suffer a loss of clarity and specificity rather than disappearing altogether with the delightful term *graceful degradation*. Reviewing photo albums and videos helps us counter this degradation. They provide a record of some of the details that have eventually become lost to our memory as a result of brain circuits slowly atrophying from disuse. But you can come up with fresh and unexpected memories many years later if you use an associative method like Bradbury's.

Whatever the precise explanation for their success, the methods espoused by both Bradbury and Joyce share a grounding in the present moment. Each writer temporarily adopted a certain degree of passivity toward his experiences; he momentarily put aside memories of the past and formulations for the future and, instead, sought inspiration solely from immediately accessible events. Neither of them was afraid of "letting go" of the past and the future in order to experience himself floating freely among the characters of his own creation. You should do the same. "Why did God make us?" a rabbi asked. "Because he likes to tell stories" came the answer. Become an active participant in your own life story. Conceptualize reality in brain terms: the art of montage.

4

Your capacity for new learning remains and may increase as you grow older.

Traditionally, neuroscientists believed that once the human brain achieved adult proportions, it remained stable over the next several decades and then underwent an inevitable decline in structure and function. They also believed that lost brain cells could never be replaced. Neither of these formerly hallowed tenets is still thought to be true.

According to recent research, brain cells continue to multiply in the hippocampus, an important center for learning and memory. In addition, the brain is not a static structure, but exhibits a remarkable plasticity over time according to the richness of a person's experience. For instance, professional musicians use more neurons in brain areas related to music when compared to the brains of nonmusicians. Even when they're just listening to music, musicians activate more neurons than nonmusicians. Although these changes vary according to the years of musical instruction, it is never too late to enhance the musical appreciation centers in the brain. Thus, if you take up a musical instrument today, your brain will undergo changes consistent with the extent of your subsequent skill and experience. Such plasticity is one of the fundamental principles of brain operation. Further, this tendency for the brain to increase in complexity can be found throughout the animal kingdom. What follows is a description of experience-based differences in the brain of the lowly fly. "Careful analyses have uncovered remarkable structural plasticity in the fly's brain, revealing that it is not only highly variable in size but that most regions are continuously reorganizing depending on the specific living conditions with which the fly is faced," according to researcher George L. Gabor Miklos, a senior fellow at the Neuroscience Institute in La Jolla, California.

Turning our attention to creatures higher on the food chain, rats, when provided with toys, companions, and more spacious living conditions, grow additional brain cells. The animals also get smarter and perform better in behavioral tests. It's likely that your brain cells will also continue to multiply in certain important areas if you continue to challenge yourself intellectually. Think of the brain as a work in progress that continues from birth until the day you die. At every moment, your activities and thoughts are modifying your brain. That modification can lead to enhanced brain performance and capabilities. This holds true no matter what your age or how late in life you begin. In one study carried out by Robert P. Friedlander of the Case Western Reserve University School of Medicine, the risk of developing Alzheimer's disease was found to be greatly diminished in those who had participated more often in intellectual activities in their twenties and thirties. But even individuals who had increased their intellectual activities in their forties or later also reduced their risk.

Nor are "intellectual activities" restricted to traditional academics. Figure D, on page 39, shows the intellectual activities that help protect against Alzheimer's disease. Included here are activities ranging from scholarly pursuits like reading and letter writing to

Figure D

ACTIVITY CATEGORIES AND ACTIVITY TYPES

Passive

Watching television

Listening to music

Attending social clubs

Talking on the telephone, visiting
with others

Attending church or synagogue
activities

Intellectual

Reading

Working on jigsaw puzzles

Working on crossword puzzles

Playing a musical instrument

Doing craft work

Painting, drawing, or creating other
art

Practicing woodworking

Writing letters

Playing cards

Playing board games

Doing handywork or home repairs

Knitting, crocheting, or doing other
needlework

Physical

Playing baseball, football,
basketball, soccer, hockey

Working out in a gym

Playing racquet sports

Riding a bicycle

Golfing, bowling

Gardening

Ice-skating, roller-skating

Jogging, swimming

Walking for exercise

games, puzzles, and activities involving manual skills, such as crocheting and knitting.

One thing we know for certain: You can reduce the chances that you will develop Alzheimer's disease or other forms of dementia if you think of education as a lifelong project; if you remain curious and inquisitive about people and events; and if you practice the exercises presented in this book. By taking active efforts to remain mentally agile, you increase both your chances of growing new nerve cells and the likelihood that your brain will maintain and increase its nerve cell connections and circuits. We know this because of positron-emission tomography (PET) scan studies carried out on intellectually gifted people.

In one PET scan study, the brain areas employed to encode the sounds made by a piano turned out to be larger in skilled musicians than in people who had never played an instrument. When piano sounds were played to both groups, the response was 25 percent greater in musicians than in nonmusicians. Further, the earlier in life that the musicians had taken up their instruments, the greater their response to the piano notes. Presumably, skilled musicians, as a result of their training, use more neurons for musical processing. They are also better at synchronizing musical notes played on the piano.

Brain changes can also result from the thoughts we choose to entertain. Your thoughts at any given moment affect your brain functioning. Just a few hours before writing this paragraph, I listened to one of my patients describe how she had been struck on the head and knocked briefly unconscious because of another person's act of carelessness. While describing the incident, she remained calm and composed until she began speaking about the "stupidity and thoughtlessness" of the person who had inadvertently injured her. At that moment her face flushed with anger and she squeezed her head between her hands in response to the sudden onset of a headache.

Many of us are like my patient and experience physical and psychological responses to the thoughts, words, and behavior of others. At a physical level, these responses are linked with chemical alterations no less powerful than those initiated by a drug. For example, PET scan studies reveal that thinking sad versus happy thoughts can change brain chemistry. And thinking angry thoughts can bring on physical symptoms, as illustrated by my patient. Along the same lines, if you believe strongly enough that a pill will help relieve certain of your uncomfortable symptoms when you are ill, your belief alone will alter your brain chemistry. Whether that alteration will be sufficient to cure you will depend upon the nature and seriousness of your illness. Drugs, placebos, and miracles involve different orders of discourse and we shouldn't confuse them.

In practical terms, all of the new research on the brain means that no matter how old you may be at this moment, it's never too late to change your brain for the better. That's because the brain is different from every other organ in our body. While the liver and the lungs and the kidneys wear out after a certain number of years, the brain gets sharper the more it's used. Indeed, it improves with use. Further, the functional properties of brain cells continue to be altered throughout adult life, depending on our life experiences. How do we know this? On the basis of experiments carried out on monkeys and brain-imaging studies of Braille learning in humans.

Neuroscientists measured the area of the cortex in the monkey's brain that responded to stimulation of its fingers. They found that if the monkey is trained to use a specific finger for a particular task and the animal repeats that task several thousand times, the number of cells in the brain representing that finger expand at the expense of the inactive cells.

This modification according to patterns of usage applies to the human brain as well and continues over our lifetimes. For instance, the same area measured in the monkey experiments was also enlarged in blind readers of Braille. That's because over time the fingertips of the Braille reader become finely attuned to the detection of subtle changes in the patterns of dots on the page that make up the Braille script. Even more fascinating, activity in the area of the brain receiving impulses from the fingertips of the Braille reader can vary over short time spans. For instance, if the Braille reader takes a weekend off from reading, then the corresponding area diminishes. When he or she returns to reading, that area enlarges once again.

So, celebrate the uniqueness of your brain. No two human brains are exactly alike; even identical twins possess physiologically different brains. That's because the sharing of an identical genetic endowment and family upbringing is balanced by differences in each twin's life experience. As a result of your unique knowledge, the size of your brain's cerebral cortex and the exact (molecular) configuration of that structure is unlike that of any other person on earth. In fact, the variation in neuronal numbers in your brain compared to the brain of another person varies by more than plus or minus 50 percent! Even more astonishing than these numbers are the figures on moment-to-moment variation within one individual. It is estimated that in the monkey, thirty thousand synapses are lost per second in the cortex during the period of sexual maturation. This truly incredible rate of neuronal turnover is a reflection of the dynamic nature of the brain's organization, which changes constantly in response to environmental variables.

The choices we make throughout our lives also play a part in altering the fundamental nature of our brain. Our moment-to-moment actions sculpt the brain's structure and functioning. Whenever we undertake new interests or activities and thereby form new networks, the numbers of receptors for the brain's chemical messengers (the neurotransmitters) increase (up-regulation) or decrease (down-regulation). Nerve cells even have the potential to start making different neurotransmitters. A dopamine-producing neuron, for instance, may start making and releasing another neurotransmitter, such as serotonin or glutamine. The end result of these modifications is a fundamentally different brain.

Initially, this concept of the brain's lifetime capacity for change is often difficult for many people to accept. This reluctance exists because brain alterations aren't subjectively appreciated until late in the process. For example, if you start taking a Russian language class, your initial learning will be slow and incremental. But over the span of a year or so, your facility with the Russian language will improve until you reach a point when you will hardly remember your initial stumbling efforts. But facility in the new language won't occur overnight, and you won't suddenly wake up one morning speaking perfect Russian. That's because a certain amount of time and effort will be required to establish the brain circuitry for that second language. And when that scaffolding is finally in place, you will experience yourself and the world differently. Suddenly you'll appreciate that well-founded aphorism "Another language, another soul."

The process of brain modification accompanying new learning, although subtler, isn't that much different from what happens in an exercise program. After sustained efforts aimed at getting in better physical shape, you begin to notice that you fit more comfortably into your clothes and tire less quickly. With the brain, of course, the changes are purely functional: you can't observe your brain changing (unless you have access to a PET scanner). But your brain *is* altering, as that PET scan image would attest. New circuits are forming all the time, depending on your level of mental activity or inactivity.

The brain also responds to stimulation differently as we get older. In the first few years of life, the brain forms its circuits by attrition. Those neurons that are recruited into the networks and "nerve nets" survive, while cells not so selected die off. Thus, the sheer number of nerve cells decreases, but the richness and complexity of brain circuitry increases. The process has been compared to the art of the stone sculptor: creation via *elimination* rather than, as with the painter, creation via the addition of materials. As we mature beyond that stage, brain cell attrition largely ceases. Instead, neurons band together into networks that increase in number, with any one neuron potentially involved in thousands of circuits. The greater number of circuits a neuron participates in the better, because while activity and use is invigorating, the absence of activity and disuse leads to stagnation and death. Additional networks can be easily formed as spin-offs from existing networks, and this is one of the reasons why learning a third or a fourth language isn't nearly as difficult as the initial learning of the second language.

The acquisition of multiple languages can go particularly rapidly if undertaken early in life, when the brain is most plastic and malleable. At this early period of development, neurons easily enter into multiple circuits. And if this interest in learning new languages is maintained over the years, neurons can be recruited into new language circuits—a situation subjectively experienced as a facility and a "gift" for languages. But if new languages aren't learned in school or elsewhere, great difficulty is experienced if attempts are made later. This situation is an example of the same principle that governs physical activities.

For instance, a professional athlete in one sport can usually manage a superior performance in another sport. Maybe Michael Jordan didn't make it as a professional baseball player, but he certainly outperformed 99 percent of "weekend" amateur baseball players. That's because those years of practice and competition in professional basketball had resulted in the development within his brain of an elaborate neuronal circuitry for superior athletic performance. In many cases, the brain circuitry for one sport can be incorporated into the circuitry required for another sport. In the absence of such circuitry (the problem with your typical couch potato), no circuit exists for modification.

Post-trauma, an adult brain shows less plasticity and is less malleable than that of a child. After brain injury, a child's brain recovers more quickly: it is a generalist with many parts capable of assuming the duties of others. The adult's brain, in contrast, is a specialist with areas less able to substitute for each other. The situation is like requiring a carpenter to do the work of an electrician or vice versa. While the right hemisphere is capable of rudimentary speech, for instance, it never performs up to the standards of the speech-specialized left hemisphere. In the adult, the specialization is sufficiently developed that the right hemisphere can never completely compensate for language deficits resulting from left hemisphere strokes. In the young child, in contrast, the entire left hemisphere can be removed and normal speech may still develop.

Fortunately, the specialization that accompanies aging is less powerful at the level of neurotransmitters and receptors. Indeed, when it comes to chemistry and function rather than structure, the brain remains highly malleable throughout your life. As you read these sentences and learn new information, neurotransmitter and receptor patterns undergo constant modification. Your previous experience determines the extent of this modification. Learn a lot and the brain circuitry changes extensively; learn little and your brain's organization remains limited to the same neuronal networks.

5

Learn about your brain's motor programs and how to use them.

Recently I spent the morning playing table tennis. While this seems like an inactive pastime compared to "real" tennis, consider the following similarities: Both games demand fine eye-hand coordination and control; both require skill in striking a ball so that it lands with an accuracy sometimes measured in millimeters; and, finally, both games reward the acquired ability to quickly and accurately assess an opponent's skills.

Of course, there are differences. The miniaturized version is far less physically demanding and (on the positive side) provides less opportunity for injury. And when playing each of these games, the brain recruits different muscle groups. For instance, the fingers and wrist play a pivotal role in table tennis, while a win at the U.S. Open requires the additional strength and vigor supplied by the muscles of the upper arms and shoulders.

In shifting back and forth from table tennis to regular full court tennis, the brain improvises from a basic motor program involving different proportions of strength and power in the arms and shoulders combined with fine control of the movements of the wrist and fingers. But this isn't unusual. The brain shifts motor programs on a regular basis. Thousands of times per day, depending on our activities and the circumstances, the brain activates different muscles that provide various combinations of power and precision.

For example, suppose you decide to go to the corner drugstore to buy a newspaper. At the moment of decision, you imagine yourself sitting comfortably in your living room reading the paper. But first you have to buy the paper. You decide to walk down the street to the drugstore and thereby get some exercise. This requires the formulation by the brain of a motor program for walking. But when you get to the front door you discover a change in the weather and heavy rain. At this point your brain modifies the motor program to include the carrying of an umbrella. But where is your umbrella? You can't recall where you last put it. After a few minutes of fruitless searching for the umbrella, you finally remember you left it at the office. With this realization you put aside all considerations about exercise and descend into the garage. Ten minutes later you arrive back home in your car with the paper.

What started out as a plan for a leisurely walk changed to a projected walk in the rain and, finally, ended up as a car trip. Each of these activities evolved from the same premotor program (buying a paper), but involved different motor programs engaging different muscle groups and different patterns of action. The rules and goals remained the same; only the means of achieving those goals changed. Your brain didn't operate according to a simple stimulus-response pattern marked by an unvarying behavioral repertoire (get the paper), but as a dynamic organ that altered its performance depending on circumstances.

It's the prefrontal lobes that engineer premotor programs. After formulating the programs, the prefrontal lobes dispatch their orders to the motor cortex and the cerebellum, which together carry out the desired action. Figure E, on page 48, is a diagram of the human brain's frontal and prefrontal lobes. Massively developed in comparison to those of other living species, this critically important area at the far front of the brain is the key to human distinctiveness. It is principally responsible for four control functions.

- **SEQUENCING.** We are capable of handling sequential information, maintaining it accurately and in proper sequence, and, finally, reorganizing it for later processing. After you've read a book, you may want to later summarize it for a friend. This will require sequencing.

- **DRIVE.** To remain alert and aware of events and people around us requires the ability to pay attention and stay focused. While people vary in their capacity to do this, children and adults with attention deficit disorder (ADD) have the greatest difficulty. Their problem, according to recent research, stems from malfunctions in the frontal lobes.

Figure E

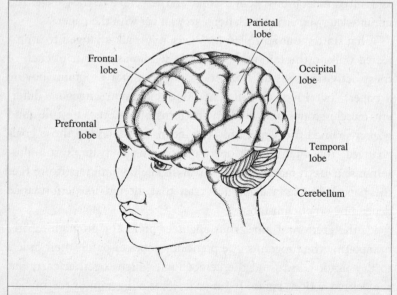

Figure E A view of the brain from the left, showing the cerebellum and the cerebral hemisphere's major divisions.

- **EXECUTIVE CONTROL.** This is what really separates us from all other higher primates. We can anticipate the potential consequences of our actions ("If I run that red light I may end up with a ticket"). We can monitor the responses we're eliciting from other people ("The boss doesn't seem to be responding very well to my lighthearted comments about our productivity problem, so maybe I better cut the comedy and get serious"). And we can simultaneously manage several different processes at once (while driving to the office I can listen to an audiobook on the tape deck in my car, think about an upcoming meeting, and still successfully maneuver through traffic).

- **FUTURE MEMORY.** Despite the strange title, the concept is easily understood. Lewis Carroll captured the essence of future memory when he wrote, "It's a poor sort of memory that only works backwards." Future memory refers to your ability to look forward to future goals and keep them in mind in the present so that current inconveniences don't sidetrack you. For instance, if you want to become a neurosurgeon you have to put in a lot of time, money, and effort before you eventually achieve your goal. During those arduous years of training, your memory of that early vision of yourself as a neurosurgeon will serve as an inspiration and a guide. People with frontal lobe disorders experience great difficulty imagining themselves in any situation other than where they are now. In a phrase, they suffer from a defect in future memory.

In essence, our frontal and prefrontal lobes are responsible for our ability to project ourselves into the future. The prefrontal lobes come up with the intention and the frontal lobes, via their motor connections, carry it out. Thanks to these humanizing brain areas, we are the only creatures that can transcend limitations of space and time. We can imagine ourselves already in possession of the things we want. And this isn't just a form of daydreaming. According to recent research on PET scans, we don't have to *do* anything in order to change our brains.

In recent years, neuroscientists have recorded PET scan images of brain activity associated with "pure thought." The technique involves comparing PET scan measurements taken during a motor activity such as a complex arm movement with PET images taken while the subject just thinks about moving the arm. Imagining the movement alone activates areas in the prefrontal cortex.

"In general the frontal and prefrontal cortex, which differs hugely in volume between humans and even our closest primate relatives, is greatly implicated in processes involving planning, choice, volition, memory, and similar cognitive functions," according to Richard S.J. Frackowiak, professor of neurology at the Institute of Neurology in London.

What are the implications of the PET studies? They provide evidence of the benefits of mental rehearsal. "Imagining a complex or skillful movement can help improve its performance," says Frackowiak. The PET scans have placed such intuitions on a firm neurological basis. For instance, the process of imagining yourself going through the motions of a complex musical or athletic performance activates brain areas that improve your performance. What an astounding thought!

And this improvement isn't limited to music or sports. Merely thinking about doing something brings about changes in the brain's patterning. PET scans reveal that the mental rehearsal of an action activates the prefrontal areas responsible for the formulation of the appropriate motor programs. And if you then mentally decide to do something a different way by employing different muscle groups (using your right instead of your left hand, for instance), the PET scan changes again.

In practical terms, this means you can benefit from the use of mental imagery. Athletes and actors have known this for years. In situations such as temporary illnesses or travel where practice is impossible, they engage in mental rehearsal. In the process, their brains establish and maintain the premotor programs that will later guide them during the actual performance. Obviously, mental rehearsal can't substitute for the real thing, but it can serve as a helpful complement.

Premotor programming also underlies all of the advice you've ever heard about the power of positive thinking. We eventually become the products of the images we entertain about ourselves. "All that we are is the result of what we have thought," according to the *Dhammapada*. This thousand-year-old aphorism anticipated future discoveries about the brain: set up the correct premotor program and the brain will do the rest. First, think about what you want to achieve. Second, come up with specific achievable steps to facilitate your goal. Finally, regularly review the steps leading to the desired goal and clearly envision yourself possessing what you desire.

Knowing about motor programs will also help you to learn most efficiently. For example, whenever you're learning or practicing a new manual skill, you're engaging your brain's primary motor cortex and prefrontal cortex. These two areas remain active during the first forty minutes of training. During this time, the prefrontal cortex is drawing up the plan of action and the motor cortex is practicing it. After you've learned the skilled movements or enhanced your performance, it's necessary for your brain to consolidate the memory for what you've learned. This takes several hours and cannot be hurried. Thus, it probably isn't a good idea to take a tennis lesson immediately after coming in from a round of golf. Before you try your hand at a second activity, you should wait for the brain to consolidate the skill acquisition memory from the first activity. If you ignore this time requirement and try to learn a second motor skill, you will create an interference effect, according to an imaging study. In other words, your brain's ongoing efforts to make a permanent record of what you've learned from the golf lesson will interfere with your efforts to improve your tennis backhand. But if you're patient and give your brain time to consolidate your improvements on the golf course, you can then successfully turn your attention to improving your tennis skills.

So keep in mind that the brain takes a certain amount of time to encode new experiences and information. Don't hurry things to the extent that encoding fails to take place or falls prey to interference effects. Each brain is different. Learn from observation and experience how best to engage your brain's motor programs.

6

Take advantage of the intimate interrelationships of learning, memory, and intelligence.

Whenever you learn something new, that knowledge enhances the number and complexity of the brain's neuronal networks. The result is an increase in brainpower. We know about this learning-memory-intelligence linkage on the basis of an exciting experiment carried out by Dr. Joe Z. Tsien, a biologist at Princeton University.

Tsien altered the gene for one of the brain's receptors and inserted it into the DNA of ordinary mouse embryos. He chose the hippocampus because that is where memories are initially encoded. It resulted in a new strain of mice called Doogies (Doogie, you may remember, was the intellectually gifted main character in the TV show *Doogie Howser, M.D.*).

After nerve cell stimulation in ordinary mice, the receptor usually remains active for about 100 thousandths of a second. But after the genetic alteration, the receptor stayed active for 250 thousandths of a second. That extra 150 thousandths of a second was responsible for a subtle but important change.

After the gene insertion, Doogies displayed not only better memory but also greater intelligence. During an SAT designed for mice, Doogies learned faster than ordinary mice. In a water-maze test, the animals had to find a hidden platform while swimming through an opaque liquid. They then had to remember the platform location over several trials. In these tests, Doogies consistently outperformed their genetically unaltered counterparts. Doogies also tended to be more curious and showed special interest in new toys put into their cages.

Since mice and humans use the same memory-encoding mechanisms, it's likely that the same rule holds for us: increase your memory and you increase your basic intelligence. And when you think about it, why should that be a surprise? An increased memory leads to easier, quicker accessing of information, as well as greater opportunities for linkages and associations. And, basically, you are what you can remember. Your identity depends on all of the events, people, and things that you can recall. To prove this, you have only to encounter a person suffering from Alzheimer's or any other disease that destroys memory. The afflicted person's speech and behavior convey puzzlement and tentativeness. "I'm never really sure what's going on," said one of my patients in the early stage of the illness. "I know most of the people around me but I get confused about what I'm supposed to be doing with them."

The best protection against developing a memory disorder? Exercising the brain's memory mechanisms. During the early years of our education, memory-enhancing exercises formed an important part of every school curriculum. In order to advance from one grade to another, we had to learn a certain amount of information and store it for periodic recall. But as we grew older and eventually left school, we could no longer count on the encouragement of teachers and others and had to assume increasing personal responsibility for exercising our memory. Now that we're adults, exercising our powers of recall, just like physical exercise, depends entirely on our own personal efforts. Unfortunately, few of us actively flex our memory "muscles" and, as a result, they frequently atrophy.

Complaints about poor memory head the list of items brought to a neurologist's office by people over forty. Fortunately, very few of these people actually suffer from neurological illnesses. Those who are not depressed (the commonest cause of subjective complaints of memory impairment) are simply experiencing the cumulative effect of decades of memory disuse. Part of this disuse is cultural. Most businesses and occupations seldom demand that their employees recite facts and figures purely from memory. In addition, in some quarters memory is even held in contempt. "He's just parroting a lot of information he doesn't really understand" is a common put-down when people are enviously criticizing someone with a powerful memory. Of course, on some occasions, such criticisms are justified, particularly when brute recall occurs in the absence of understanding or context. But I'm not advocating brute recall. I'm suggesting that, starting now, you aim for a superpowered memory, a memory aimed at quicker, more accurate retrieval of information.

Prior to the development of the printing press, when the technology of information transfer was limited to the production of handwritten copies, facts had to be memorized and passed on via an oral tradition. The Homeric epics, *The Odyssey* and *The Iliad*, were recited at Greek festivals and celebrations by professional singers called rhapsodes who marked the measures with rhythm staffs. Some scholars even claim Homer never actually wrote down his poems but recounted them strictly from memory. Whether or not this is true, singers and poets for several hundred years before Homer memorized and recited the stories that formed the basis for Homer's epic cycle. During those periods, the brain had to work harder; as a result, superpowered memories were not all that unusual.

Today, technology both helps and hinders the development of a superpowered memory. As I will discuss in more detail in chapter 27, you should think of the technology of pens, paper, tape recorders, computers, and electronic diaries as an extension of the brain. Thanks to these aids, we can carry incredible amounts of information around with us. While this increase in readily available information is generally beneficial, there is also a downside. The storage and rapid retrieval of information from a computer also exerts a stunting effect on our brain's memory capacities. But we can overcome this by working to improve our memory by aiming at the development and maintenance of a superpowered memory. In the process of improving our powers of recall, we will strengthen our brain circuits, starting at the hippocampus and extending to every other part of our brain.

Before proceeding to some brain-related approaches to memory improvement, consider this question: What kind of memory improvement do you seek? Would you like to remember absolutely everything that ever happened to you? A man with a perfect memory actually existed and formed the basis for a fascinating book, *The Mind of a Mnemonist*, written by Russian psychologist Aleksandr Luria.

At age thirty, when Luria first encountered him, "S." could remember long series of words, letters, or numbers. When reexamined for these lists sixteen years later, S. was able to repeat the original sequences without error. Moreover, he could do this in reverse order just as readily—an indication that he employed eidetic imagery ("photographic memory"). Over a period covering almost thirty years of testing, Luria came to the conclusion that "the span of his memory had no distinct limits." Is this the kind of memory that you desire? Before you answer "Yes" to that question, let me provide you with a little more information about S.

Rather than proving a blessing, S.'s phenomenal memory worked against him. Since he remembered everything, he found it difficult to put events into perspective. In fact, he couldn't even stick to the point in a conversation. "His remarks would be cluttered with details and irrelevancies; he would become verbose, digress endlessly, and finally have to strain to get back to the subject of the conversation," wrote Luria. Over his lifetime S. achieved little benefit from his perfect memory and died an unfulfilled, unhappy man who considered himself a failure.

Judging from S.'s experience, maybe it isn't such a great thing to possess a perfect memory. So what kind of enhanced memory do you desire? A superpowered memory seems like a reasonable goal. And most of us would like a greater sense of control over our memory so that we can confidently bring to mind whatever it is that we want to remember.

At this point, let's try some elementary exercises that test different kinds of memory. First let's work to improve immediate recall (short-term memory). Write down a series of numbers selected at random. Start with strings of five digits and work up to nine digits. Don't think about the numbers; just quickly write whatever comes to mind. Now, without looking at the numbers, repeat the string of digits either aloud or in your mind at a rate of one per second. When you can repeat nine digits without error, increase the number of digits until you reach your personal outer limit. At this point, return to the five-digit strings and recite the numbers *backward*. After some practice, you should be able to manage at least nine digits. If you begin to falter and you're not certain of the correctness of your performance, do the exercise with a tape recorder. Start reciting and keep going until you've finished. Then rewind the tape and check whether you made some of the more common errors, such as reversing numbers toward the middle of the string.

Next, perform the exercise with words instead of numbers. After spelling the word correctly in the forward direction, try spelling it backward. You can even skip the forward recitation here since that is more a test of spelling than of memory. Start with an easy one like *hospital* (latipsoh), and work with the following list: *complete, register, nonpareil, university, idiosyncrasy, Winchester, rudderless,* and *onomatopoeia*. See the word clearly in your mind and repeat it until you can accurately recite it backward. After successfully reciting these words, you should make up another list drawn from your daily reading. Eliminate a word from the list when you have mastered it. Replace that word with another encountered during your reading. Some words you will recognize immediately as a difficult challenge (a proper name like Carl von Clauswitz); some words you may not be capable of reversing despite your best efforts. But don't become discouraged; the goal is not to compete against other people, but to enhance your immediate recall and short-term memory. If you encounter an interesting word during your reading, try spelling it backward. If you have trouble, add the word to your regularly updated list of words for short-term memory testing.

The next exercise aims at enhancing new learning ability. Select four unrelated words (such as red, loyalty, narcissus, eyeglasses) and write them down. Study the words for fifteen seconds and then put them away. Set an alarm for five minutes (I use a wristwatch alarm in order to give me maximum mobility) and continue with some other activity. Totally focus your attention on whatever activity you're engaged in at the moment. Most important, don't rehearse the words. When the alarm sounds, recall the four words in any order. Change the words: for example, whistle, library, needle, courage. Set the alarm for thirty minutes and go on to other activities. When the alarm sounds, try to recall the words. With each success, increase the number of words and the time frame until you get to about ten words remembered over several hours. It's important in this exercise that you don't attempt to link or associate the words. Simply register the words without any conscious attempts to form memory "pegs" (i.e., "it takes *courage* to blow a *whistle* in a *library* after accidentally sticking oneself with a *needle*"). The use of such pegs involves another form of memory, which we will discuss in the next chapter.

Here is a related but more challenging exercise. Review the list of fifteen randomly selected words in the far left-hand column of Figure F on page 59. Then read the words slowly into a tape recorder. When you're finished, see how many of them you can write down in the column labeled Trial I, in any order that occurs to you. Don't look at the original list; rather, rewind the tape and listen to yourself reading it once again. Then write in the column labeled Trial II all the words that you can remember. Repeat this exercise three more times, for a total of five trials written out in five columns. With each repetition you should remember more words, but in five tries can you come up with all of the words?

Next, select and read into the tape recorder a second list (called the interference list). A sample list has been provided in Figure F on page 60. After hearing the words from that list, write down as many words as you can remember in the column labeled Trial VI. Now, without listening again to the first list, see how many words you can recall and write them in the column labeled Trial VII. You'll find that until you become practiced at this exercise, words from the interference list will "intrude" and lessen the accuracy of your remembrance of the first list.

At this point, set your alarm for five minutes and relax. When the alarm sounds, write down as a test of delayed recall all of the words from the original list that you listened to for a total of five times.

Finally, in a test of your recognition memory, have someone make up a list of words composed of the original list intermixed with an equal number of distracter words that haven't appeared before. Circle only those words you are certain you actually recognize. And be forewarned of a mental quirk that may interfere with the accuracy of your recall. Related words often trick the brain into false recognition. For instance, since the words *finger, watch,* and *pen* appeared on the original list, your brain may be fooled into selecting words like *thumb, clock,* and *pencil*.

After you have mastered the above exercise, try a harder variation. Ask somebody else to select the words for the original and the distracter lists and read them for you into the tape recorder. That eliminates the chance that you may be falsely augmenting your memory performance by unconsciously selecting favored or frequently used words. In addition, hearing someone else's voice rather than your own increases the challenge of the exercise. You don't hear yourself saying the words in a kind of inner echo chamber.

Another, more natural, exercise in new learning involves the use of Cliff's Notes or other available book summaries. Choose a book that you have read sometime in the past. After reading a summary of

Figure F

OBJECT	TRIAL I	TRIAL II	TRIAL III	TRIAL IV	TRIAL V
1. Pen					
2. Cauliflower					
3. Wine					
4. Key					
5. Auditorium					
6. Wish					
7. Tent					
8. Pin					
9. Finger					
10. Ring					
11. Chair					
12. Watch					
13. Sieve					
14. Telephone					
15. Cart					

TRIAL	I	II	III	IV	V	TOTAL
Correct:						
Repeats:						
Errors:						

Figure F *(continued)*

	TRIAL VI
1. Toe	
2. Monkey	
3. Sun	
4. Tea	
5. Clarinet	
6. Cabin	
7. Sailor	
8. Church	
9. Screen	
10. Lamp	
11. Robe	
12. Window	
13. Spoon	
14. Witch	
15. Vase	

Correct:	
Repeats:	
Errors:	

	TRIAL VII
1. Pen	
2. Cauliflower	
3. Wine	
4. Key	
5. Auditorium	
6. Wish	
7. Tent	
8. Pin	
9. Finger	
10. Ring	
11. Chair	
12. Watch	
13. Sieve	
14. Telephone	
15. Cart	

Correct:	
Repeats:	
Errors:	

a chapter, dictate into your recorder everything you can remember about it. Your goal is to come up with correct memories for every detail. For instance, here is the summary for Part III, chapter 4 of one of my favorite novels, *Crime and Punishment*:

> **The family reunion of the Raskolnikovs is interrupted by the appearance of Sonya. Rodya offers her a seat and tells her to sit between his mother and his sister. She has come to invite him, in fact to entreat him for Katerina Ivanovna's sake, to be present at the funeral and afterwards at a funeral lunch. Suddenly Sonya feels extremely embarrassed because she realizes due to the poverty of his room that Raskolnikov must have given them everything.**

Your recollection should include every specific detail (a family reunion, the names, where Sonya sat, her purpose in coming, her observation, and her conclusion).

Next, test your immediate recall skills for spoken rather than written material. Ask someone to record some chapter summaries read slowly and carefully. Later, you can play back the reading and test your memory until you can correctly recall every detail.

After that, move on to a test for paired associated learning. First, write down a list of twenty word pairs. The words should be chosen at random. I get my words by fanning through a dictionary and linking randomly encountered words (fuddled, graith). Try to avoid obvious linkages (book, page; high, low) and, as an added benefit of the exercise, learn the meaning of all unfamiliar words. When you have a list of twenty word pairs, study it for five minutes and then cover the first word of the pairs and see how many of the associated words you can recall.

Next, select at random three letters of the alphabet and write them at the top of a column. Set your timer and speak into your tape recorder as many words beginning with that letter that you can think of in one minute. Don't hesitate or censor in any way (naughty words are okay just as long as they are, indeed, words). When you're finished, write out your list in the columns. To get a feeling for this test and its power, start off with a variation.

Instead of letters, quickly list on the tape recorder as many animal names as you can remember in one minute. When finished, write the names in a column labeled "Animals." The normal performance for anyone under seventy years old is between seventeen and twenty-four animal names. When you're finished, repeat the test with a change in your strategy. Think about ways of categorizing animals (domesticated, undomesticated, pets, found on farms, found in zoos, dangerous, four-footed, flying, crawling, swimming, etc.). With these categories in mind, repeat the test. You should notice a measurable improvement based on an elementary principle of brain operation. The brain operates at its best when working within a context and when provided with structure and meaning. Even listing the first two or three animals that come to mind beginning with successive letters of the alphabet will improve your performance as long as you move on to the next letter the instant you can't come up with the name of another animal starting with a particular letter. Next, try lists of tools, movie star names, famous authors—you select the category. In each instance, you are strengthening verbal fluency—the only language function, incidentally, that tends to diminish with age.

The exercises described so far challenge the left hemisphere, which deals with words and numbers. Here is an exercise that challenges the right hemisphere. Memorize the designs in Figure G, on pages 63 and 64. Don't think or inwardly talk about them; just look at the designs and after a few minutes draw what you saw from memory. Next, make some designs of your own and see if you can reproduce them a few minutes later. The initial goal is to achieve general accuracy. Later, you will aim at reproducing the original drawing with sufficient precision that the drawings can be superimposed on each other (a level of performance that nonartists and "left hemisphere types" may never achieve, so don't become discouraged).

Simpler visual memory exercises can be performed at any time and don't require any equipment other than your eyes and brain. Memorize the layout of a room or the seating arrangement at a table. After a few minutes, close your eyes or look away and see if you

can mentally re-create it. Then make a rough sketch of the room and put in as many items as you can "see" in your mind's eye. For an additional challenge, try memorizing something that involves both words and spatial arrangement. For instance, try memorizing the titles of a row of books on the nearby shelf. When you close your eyes, try to "see" them, envisioning both the book titles and their arrangement on the shelf.

As another exercise in visual imagery—this one incorporating dynamic rather than static images—record a favorite television program. After the show, play back *in your mind* each of the scenes. Envision each scene clearly and precisely. If you do it correctly, the whole show should unfold in your imagination as if you had fast-forwarded the video. In this exercise, allow your brain to function like the television monitor: all criticism and commentary are suspended as you simply watch and listen. With practice you should be able to re-create at fast-forward speed an entire half-hour program.

Next, bring the left hemisphere into the exercise. If the show is a drama, aim for a shorthand summary of events, important dialogue, and the actions of the principal characters. If you've watched a documentary instead, set down a chronological reconstruction of the human interest stories, vignettes, and interviews employed to make the show's main points. When you've finished this mental exercise, replay the show and see how well you did. Finally, since it's unlikely you'll want to watch the same show for a third time, erase the video and repeat the exercise at another time with a different program.

Initially, you will find many of the above brain-memory exercises as tiring as vigorous physical activity. That's because the brain, along with every other organ in the body, responds to challenge by requiring increased amounts of blood, oxygen, and glucose. And as with any bodily process involving energy and its expenditure, fatigue is a natural consequence. But keep up your efforts. The going gets easier with regular practice. Soon you'll be finding memory exercises enjoyable and relaxing. Best of all, they can be practiced at any time.

Standing in a long line at the supermarket? Don't drift off into a funk. Instead, form a mental snapshot of the people in the adjoining line. Include details such as their dress and general appearance. Turn away, mentally re-create your "snapshot," and then look back to check the accuracy of your memory.

7

Improve your memory by using a memory system.

In this chapter, we'll discuss specific techniques that enable you to further improve your memory performance. First, if you want a superpowered memory, keep in mind an important memory principle first set down in 1956 by George Miller, a Princeton University psychologist. In a famous paper titled "The Magical Number Seven, Plus or Minus Two," Miller revived and tested an observation dating to nineteenth-century Scottish philosopher William Hamilton.

The philosopher noted that after throwing a handful of marbles on a floor, "you will find it difficult to view at once more than six, or seven at most, without confusion." But more items can be remembered, commented Hamilton, when they are coded or "chunked." One can remember long strings of numbers, letters, or words when they are reconstructed into meaningful patterns, also known as "memory pegs."

For instance, the position of the planets in relation to the Sun can be remembered by the mnemonic (memory aid) "My

Very Educated Mother Just Sent Us Nine Pizzas," which serves as a reminder of the planetary sequence: Mercury, Venus, Earth, Mars, Jupiter, Saturn, Uranus, Neptune, and Pluto. Another mnemonic, "On Old Olympic's Towering Tops a Finn and German Vied at Hops," helps medical students recall the names of the twelve cranial nerves, starting with the olfactory and working down to the hypoglossal.

Historically, chunking often accounted for many inexplicable and seemingly marvelous memory performances. Possibly the most famous example is that of Mozart's memorization of the *Miserere* written more than a century earlier by the Italian composer Gregorio Allegri. In 1770, while in his early teens, Mozart visited the Vatican's Sistine Chapel and heard this choral work performed on only two occasions. He then sat down and wrote out the entire score from memory. We know this because only three copies of the score existed at the time and its owner, the Vatican, forbade any publication. Thus, Mozart had no source for re-creating the score other than his own recall of the performances he had attended.

Now that the score is freely available, Mozart's accomplishment seems less remarkable. Musicians have told me that the *Miserere* is harmonically quite conventional for the period. Anyone who shared Mozart's familiarity with similar musical forms would not find it a great challenge to chunk large parts of the work around these standard structures.

"Mozart's feat of memory does not involve inexplicable processes which set him apart from other musicians," writes John Sloboda in *The Musical Mind*. "Rather it distinguishes him as someone whose superior knowledge and skill allow him to accomplish something rapidly and supremely confidently which most of us can do, albeit less efficiently, and on a smaller scale."

While Sloboda's claim seems a bit extravagant, there is no doubt that one's memory can be improved by special knowledge, efficient processing, or the application of special memory techniques that incorporate chunking.

My favorite instructional book on memory is titled simply *The*

Memory Book, by the late mnemonist (memory expert) and magician Harry Lorrayne and former NBA player Jerry Lucas. They suggest a chunking method based on the ancient "method of places" first suggested by a Greek poet, Simonides of Ceos. This involved an imaginary walk through one's own house or town square. At selected locations along the walk, Simonides would conjure up a vivid mental picture of the location to remind him of a point he wished to make in a speech.

In essence, the memory method involved linking what one wished to memorize with a specific location and a vivid image. The reason for the use of vivid images was first provided by the unknown author of *Ad Herennium,* the oldest memory book in the world (written ca. 82 B.C.). In it, the author wrote that "ordinary things easily slip from the memory while the striking and the novel stay longer in the mind. We ought then to set up images that can adhere longest in memory. And we shall do so if we establish similitudes as striking as possible; if we set up images that are not many or vague but active; if we assign to them exceptional beauty or singular ugliness."

In practice, the thing to be remembered is associated with a vivid mental picture. This picture is then imaginatively placed within some familiar setting, such as a room in one's home. The "art of memory" consists of mentally touring, say, the living room and observing the remembered objects occupying familiar places, such as a chair or a mantelpiece or a vase of flowers. In general, the more stark and vivid the image the easier its recall.

To try the method yourself, close your eyes and picture a room in your house or apartment where you spend a lot of time. After you have imaged as many things as you can, open your eyes, look around the room, and check the accuracy and completeness of your mental picture. Repeat this process until you can faithfully reproduce the main objects in the room well enough for you to walk your mind through the room. In some cases, this may take several hours of practice carried out over three or four sessions. The goal is to envision the components of the room with the utmost clarity and accuracy. When you can do that, use the mental images of the objects, places, and areas in the room as "hooks" for placing the things you're trying to remember. As you mentally stroll past a specific article of furniture, you'll see sitting there one of the objects on the list you've memorized.

A complementary memory method involves linking together dramatic and often bizarre images that represent the memorized material. In their book, Lorrayne and Lucas give several examples of the use of stark images to provide memory clues to overcome absentmindedness. For instance, if you want to be sure you don't leave your umbrella at the office, they suggest the following "ridiculous" image: "As you arrive and put your umbrella away, associate it to the first thing you see or do as you're leaving the office. If you ride in an elevator picture an umbrella operating it."

But whichever of the two memory systems you select (I recommend a combination of both), start your efforts to recall with something that stirs your interest. This might be poetry; the places, dates, and names associated with famous battles; the performance statistics of favorite athletes; the states and their capitals; the presidents; or perhaps key passages from the works of Shakespeare. In each instance, check written information only after you have tried to remember it on your own. Follow the same procedure for more mundane matters, such as supermarket lists. Memorize your list and don't look at it until you can't remember any more items from the list and it's time to proceed to the checkout counter.

At this point, return to the memory challenges presented in chapter 6 and learn and apply one of the memory-enhancing aids listed in the back of the book under "Resources." I recommend both *Memory Power: Memory-Building Skills for Everyday Situations* and *The Memory Pack: Everything You Need to Know to Supercharge Your Memory and Master Your Life.* Either of these programs will enable you to increase your memory power. Combine one or both of these programs with a reading of *The Seven Sins of Memory,* by psychologist Daniel Schacter. He discusses the seven major impediments to achieving a finely honed memory and how to overcome them. The impediments are bias, absentmindedness, transience, blocking, mis-attribution, suggestibility, and persistence.

So far we have talked principally about verbal language–based exercises that primarily challenge the left hemisphere. Now let's try some visualization exercises that challenge the right hemisphere, where images are mediated. Best of all, the following exercises require no special knowledge and can be done anywhere at any time.

At this moment, close your eyes and mentally envision the room in which you are reading this book. Don't look around first and then close your eyes: do it *right now*. After picturing everything you can remember, open your eyes and check for accuracy. Repeat the process—only this time go for the little details like the exact number and identity of the magazines lying on the coffee table. Then repeat the process again and pursue greater levels of detail. If you have already performed the earlier exercise of memorizing the outline and contents of a room in your house, this exercise should come easily to you.

As an alternative exercise, take an imaginary walk in front of your bookshelf and picture each title and its placement on the shelf. While carrying out this exercise, make a special effort not to engage in any internal dialogues with yourself about how well you're doing. Remember: this is a visualization exercise.

After a few minutes of mentally creating these increasingly detailed images you'll begin to feel slightly uncomfortable: a mix of fatigue and mild anxiety. Try to ignore these feelings and delve deeper. When you finally reach the limit of your power for pictorial recall, open your eyes and simply stare at the scene for a few more moments. At that point, your brain will bring into play language-mediated responses: "Of course, there is a small crack along that window ledge. Why didn't I see that?" or *"The Count of Monte Cristo* is actually to the right rather than to the left of *Hard Times."*

Such left-hemisphere responses underscore the holistic nature of brain functioning. The brain integrates the different operations carried out by the right and left hemispheres into one total experience.

Visualization exercises strengthen the powers of the right hemisphere. And when you bring the left hemisphere into play, the integration between the hemispheres is enhanced.

As an aid in enhancing your visualization memory powers, start carrying a disposable camera with you. When places and situations pique your interest, take a few photographs. Later, during a visualization session, you can check the accuracy of your internal image of these engaging scenes against the details revealed in the photograph.

Asian art, especially Tibetan Buddhist paintings, was created to enhance the powers of visual perception. Buddhist devotees intensely studied the paintings until they could envision the images down to the smallest detail. They believed this act of visualization and intense concentration cleansed and prepared their minds to assume the attributes and wisdom of the beings portrayed in the paintings. In the words of Roberta Smith, a *New York Times* art critic, "These images are visual exercises of the highest order. Each time you look at them, you see and understand more. . . . They were often tools that helped develop the powers of meditation basic to enlightenment." If Tibetan art doesn't interest you, memorize the scenes depicted by Western artists such as Velázquez and Hieronymus Bosch, who are noted for their renderings of finely detailed and variegated images.

At some point, you will be ready for visual exercises involving moving patterns. These pose the greatest challenge. "*Akasa*" games, as they are termed in Asia, are played by "imagining a board in the air." Mental chess is the predominant *akasa* game in our culture. Most chess masters can manage a game of "mental chess"; some of the great masters of the past could play several opponents simultaneously while blindfolded. If you play chess—and you should if you're serious about acquiring and maintaining a mental edge—here's an *akasa* exercise to try. Although it's less demanding than blindfold chess, you'll find it challenging.

Read into a tape recorder the first dozen moves of a famous chess match. My favorite is the game played in 1858 by American chess prodigy Paul Morphy against Duke Karl Brunswick and Count

Isouard during an intermission in the royal box at the opera house in Paris. Whichever game you choose, read the moves slowly and distinctly with a five-second pause between each move. (For the first few efforts, you probably won't have to read more than a dozen moves.) Then set up the chessboard and begin.

Turn on the tape recorder and *mentally* make the first move by white, followed by black's response. Image the resulting position of the pieces on the board. Continue the moves until you experience a slight lack of clarity or doubt about the position of the pieces. Focus as keenly as possible. *See* the pieces in your mind. When you reach the point where you can't image the board and the position of the pieces, open your eyes and move the pieces until you reach the position where you began to lose clarity. (The best arrangement of all is to have someone moving the pieces as you call out each move; thus, upon opening your eyes, you immediately encounter the exact position where your imaging faltered.) When you can once again establish a clear image of the position, close your eyes again and continue.

If you're not into chess, try completing a crossword puzzle without resorting to pencil or pen. As you come up with the correct words, visualize them on the grid and retain them in your memory. See how far you can get before you have to stop. Since this is a test of visualization rather than a test of your talent for solving crossword puzzles, have the solution readily at hand so you can mentally fill in the missing words and go on with visualizing. For instance, you can work on the puzzle from yesterday's paper while checking your accuracy against the solution provided in today's paper.

With these exercises, you'll be priming the frontal lobes (which govern concentration and focus), the visual association areas, and the hippocampus and its attendant connections (which govern memory).

8

Develop your emotional memory.

No matter how strong or weak your memory for facts, people, and events, there is another aspect of memory that you should seek to enhance. I'm referring here to the associated emotions that accompanied the original experience.

As an example of what I mean by emotional memory, imagine that I'm in possession of some pictures of you taken in various situations over the past year (nothing monumental, compromising, or embarrassing; just everyday pictures). Imagine further that I've put these pictures in an album and we are paging through the album together. We're starting with the pictures from yesterday and paging backward to the pictures taken a year ago.

At a certain point in this exercise, you'll start to notice a loss of your sense of emotional continuity. In other words, you will experience increasing difficulty in linking your present feelings with the feelings and emotions that existed at the moment depicted in the picture. Although you recognize yourself in the picture and can probably provide some information about what was going on at the time, you're somehow disconnected and unable to reexperience your thoughts and feelings from that past moment. And isn't that loss of emotional continuity with earlier events too important a part of your memory to relinquish? Indeed, what could be more important than your present ability to recall what was going on emotionally at the time a particular picture was taken?

If we allow our emotional memories to disappear, we eventually lose touch with ourselves. If things progress far enough, we encounter a stranger staring back at us from our mirror. I first realized this several years ago when, in an attempt to jog the failing memory of an Alzheimer's patient, I encouraged her to page with me through one of her albums of family pictures. Even in those instances when she could identify herself along with the other people in the pictures, she couldn't remember how she felt or what she had been thinking at the time. In fact, she experienced no emotional memory linkage with that former self.

Although my patient's emotional memory was grievously impaired (in some instances she couldn't identify anyone in the picture, much less the feelings she was experiencing at that time), most of us experience a less dramatic loss of continuity with our past. Fortunately, there are steps you can take to enhance your experienced memory. They are drawn from the theater, and I first learned about them from my oldest daughter, Jennifer, who is an actress.

In order to express the emotions appropriate to a given character, actresses and actors often focus on an earlier experience of the same emotion drawn from their own lives. They intuitively realize that the only way to convincingly portray an emotion is to remember and relive that emotion by recalling an experience from their own past. The same principle holds true both on and off the stage.

The best way to relive in memory emotional events from your past is to establish some emotional connection of the event with your present circumstance. Emotional memory involves momentarily experiencing yourself as you were at a certain time while simultaneously retaining your present awareness and subjectivity. Your ability to do this depends on an elementary operating principle in the brain.

Over the years, your brain constructs an internal map of your body referred to as the "body image." To experience your body image, stand in front of a full-length mirror and close your eyes. With a little effort on your part you can still "see" in your imagination how you appeared a moment earlier while looking into the mirror. Now, with your eyes still closed, raise both of your arms in front of you and then move them outward so that they form a straight line (the position assumed by a tightrope walker when balancing himself). Then, with your arms still fully extended, bring the tips of your forefingers together in front of you so that they touch. You're able to do this thanks to your brain's ability to formulate a dynamic representation of your body and, with your eyes closed and on the basis of that body image, guide your arm, hand, and finger movements in space.

As we age, our body image changes in tandem with the bodily alterations that accompany aging. For instance, a runner approaching a hurdle programs his jump based on such body image components as his height, weight, and general bodily flexibility. Several years later he will probably be slower, a bit heavier, and less flexible. Based on these physical changes, his brain will have constructed a new body image and it will program the jump differently. But changes in body image can also occur over much briefer periods of time, even over the space of just a few seconds.

As a demonstration of the malleability of the body image, sit at a table across from a partner. Place one of your hands under the table, resting palm down on your knee. Then ask your partner to tap, touch, or stroke with their fingertips the back of your hidden hand while simultaneously making the same pattern of movement on the tabletop directly above your hand. While this is going on, it's important that you concentrate your attention on the table and forget about your hand hidden from view beneath the table. If you can successfully focus on the table, you will experience something very odd after a few minutes. You will find that the table starts to feel like part of your body—as though your hand is somehow incorporated into the table. The tapping on your hand will seem to emerge from the table. In this trick, your brain has been fooled into concluding that the sensation you're feeling on your hand was produced by the action you observed taking place on the table. In order for this sensory illusion to take place, however, the synchrony must be exact: the trick fails if the pattern of movements on the table and your hand are not perfectly synchronized.

If, as a conclusion to this table experiment, your partner hits the table sharply with a hammer or other blunt object, you will likely start and register a strong galvanic skin response (a change in the electrical activity of the skin surface). But such a response will only occur if your partner's tapping on your hand and on the table take place in perfect synchrony.

"This exercise illustrates that the brain's body image is amazingly plastic," according to neurologist Vilayanur Ramachandran, who first told me about this table trick. "Even though we've all grown up with a fairly stable body image our brain assimilates the table into that image after only a few minutes of engaging in the table exercise."

With this background information on the body schema, you're now ready to try a few exercises in emotional memory arousal. To put it simply, your best chance of arousing emotional memory is by taking advantage of your brain's ability to temporarily alter your body image. Your goal in the following exercise will be to temporarily trick your brain into reformulating the body image that existed ten years ago. In the process, you will also experience some of the emotions you felt at the time.

The first exercise step in reestablishing emotional connections between past and present consists, literally, of a smoke-and-mirror trick. The aim is to make you appear like you did ten years ago. If it works for you, you will be able to merge present and past perceptions and states of consciousness.

Stand in front of a mirror in a dimly lit room (I prefer candlelight, since the illumination changes subtly from moment to moment). Place your open palms on your cheeks and firmly pull the skin upward toward the angles where the jaws articulate with the temporal bones of the skull (the temporo-mandibular joints). Hold that position and if you are 35 or older you will see yourself in the mirror as you looked 10 years ago.

As you gaze at yourself in the mirror, let your mind wander and free-associate. In the first few minutes, you might experience the temporary exhilaration reported by people who have undergone cosmetic surgery. But your purpose is different from simply wishing to appear younger. Rather, you're using the exercise to imaginatively re-create and reexperience your earlier self.

While staring into the mirror, think of your life circumstances when you looked like you do now in the mirror. For instance, if your children are now young adults, picture them as they looked when you looked like the person looking out at you from the mirror. Incidentally, don't dwell on regrets about the past; the purpose isn't to induce nostalgia or sadness. Simply try to enter into the persona looking out at you from the mirror. With sufficient concentration, you'll become aware after a few moments of random thoughts and images from ten years ago. Moreover this imaginative re-creation of the past will occur with a vividness and immediacy that rarely accompanies simple recall.

Eventually, these random thoughts and images will be accompanied by emotions—in some instances, very intense ones. These emotions are stimulated by the brain's attempt to reconcile and synthesize the disparity in facial appearance between the "you" that existed prior to this experiment, and the new "you" in the mirror. Don't try to correct or otherwise influence the process. If you are successful, your brain will begin to shift back and forth between the two states in a process similar to what happens when you look at an ambiguous figure like the Salem girl/witch (see Figure H, on page 79). Initially, you may see only one of the images or experience difficulty switching from one image to the other. Some people can't make the switch at all until the images are described (the Salem girl looks toward her right shoulder while the witch, seen in profile, possesses a large nose and an eye formed from the ear of the Salem girl). One moment the perception of a girl dominates; an instant later you're seeing a witch. Both cannot be perceived simultaneously. Similarly, your brain will not be able to process simultaneously your new and altered face in the mirror with the face that was present just the moment before you started this exercise.

On the basis of your experiences during the past ten years, your brain has incorporated within its neuronal networks a certain body image. In this exercise, the brain's current body image is different from the earlier body image of ten years ago that includes the face staring back at you. And while the brain knows the face in the mirror isn't the "real you," it still responds from moment to moment as if it were real. Most important, the memories elicited by this exercise will be suffused with vivid emotions that will bring those memories to life. You won't just remember events; you'll also remember how you *felt* about those events. To bring the exercise to a close, simply look away from the mirror and remove your hands from your face.

Incidentally, I wouldn't recommend you carry out this exercise on a frequent basis. Like all illusions, its effectiveness eventually ceases: the brain "catches on" and, in the absence of novelty and surprise, the recovered memories are experienced less vividly.

Figure H

Figure H The Salem girl/witch—a figure that can be seen either as a young girl turning her head toward her right or as a witch seen in profile.

A similar but less emotionally demanding transformation can be carried out if you have access to equipment that can perform a computerized photographic technique called morphing. This technique involves the step-by-step transformation of a photo of yourself into another photo taken many years earlier.

First, the photographs are laser-scanned. The reflected laser light from each photo is detected by a sensor that "reads" the different light levels and converts each into a digital code readable on the computer by image-manipulating software. Morphing involves shifting segments (pixels) from one photo image to another and thereby gradually effecting a transformation. Within seconds, and with only a few keystrokes, you can add or subtract decades from your photographic likeness. Even more important, you are controlling the morphing process—you are imaginatively reexperiencing and redefining yourself.

Perhaps at this point you may be wondering, "How do such exercises in temporary self-modification and self-experiencing enhance memory and intellectual performance?" The process is indirect. It involves overcoming one of the principal impediments to optimum brain functioning: our tendency to get locked into fixed ways of thinking and experiencing. This is particularly true in regard to our emotions. We literally lose touch with how we felt in the past. We feel a certain way today and tend to assume that we have always felt that way.

For instance, although all of us have gone through the turmoil of adolescence, very few of us can reexperience the accompanying emotions that we felt at the time. This failure is at least partly responsible for intergenerational conflicts. As adult men or women, we can no longer imaginatively reexperience via emotional memory how we felt decades earlier. We lack the ability to "enter into" the dreams, insecurities, and desires experienced by a teenage son or daughter. The real downside to such inflexibility comes from the ensuing developmental blockage: we can no longer communicate with our earlier self; the thoughts and feelings and desires of those earlier times are lost to us. As a result, we lose the opportunity for self-integration. The solution to such an impasse involves developing ways of reintegrating present and past selves. We cover some of these methods in this book. They can involve diaries, journals, videos, still photos, and imaginative, playful experiments such as the mirror exercise described above. The goal is to tear down the artificial and confining inner partitions that stand in the way of your optimal brain functioning.

The second exercise requires a partner and aims at enhancing emotional memory by sharpening your skills at "reading" emotions in yourself and others. Principally, the right hemisphere carries this out. We know this because people with damage to the right hemisphere often have difficulty correctly identifying and responding to other people's emotions. They seem curiously oblivious to expressions of anger, hostility, and resentment whether conveyed by word, countenance, or gesture. I'm sure you can bring to mind some friend or acquaintance afflicted with a mild form of this disorder. Some people seem incapable of perceiving the emotional states and intentions of others.

One of the difficulties in reading other people's emotions springs, of course, from the fact that we all learned early in life that we should conceal our emotions and not readily display them or talk about them to others. As a result of this inbred emotional reticence, the reading of other people's emotions from their facial expressions is a subtle and arcane art that not everyone learns successfully. The following exercise provides an antidote. It was suggested to me by some PET scan findings that indicate that when a person pretends an emotion, he or she activates the same brain areas that would be activated in circumstances when the emotions are naturally and spontaneously expressed.

Sit on the floor about three feet across from a friend. Ask her to close her eyes. Then, while gazing into her face, ask her to think about the saddest moment in her life. She shouldn't speak or otherwise respond by sighing, touching, or frowning. Study her face for the subtle changes that accompany her recall of the sad experience. After a minute, ask her to clear her mind and think of nothing in particular. She can envision anything she wants as long as it isn't emotionally arousing in any way. Observe any facial changes that may occur as her thoughts shift from sad to neutral. At this point, ask your friend to open her eyes and look directly into your eyes. Ask her once again to think about her saddest experience, then of an emotionally neutral experience, and finally her happiest experience. Keep focused on her face, particularly her eyes as she shifts from one internal experience to the other. What changes do you observe?

In the second part of the exercise, shift roles. Let your partner observe you first with your eyes closed as you think sad, indifferent, and happy thoughts. Then open your eyes and repeat the sequence. At this point in the exercise, both of you should spend one minute mentally organizing your impressions. Then share your observations and impressions.

What did you observe in her and how does it compare to what she tells you about her observations of you during the same exercise? Does hearing the details of what she was thinking enrich your observations in any way? While she's speaking of the sad experience, try to see once again those earlier changes in her eyes and face. Can you now detect something in her eyes or facial expression that escaped you when you were observing her a moment ago? Listen closely while she describes how you appeared to her when you were recalling the saddest and happiest moments in your life.

In the event that nothing seems to be happening during the exercise, remind yourselves that each of you must forgo any attempts to inhibit or control your facial expression. Both of you must remain psychologically undefended, vulnerable. It's also important that during the eyes-open part of the exercise you continue to maintain firm but gentle eye contact; not the eye contact of a salesperson or an interviewer, but that of a curious child who remains relaxed and open to a new experience. You're not trying to "stare down" your partner, but intuitively enter into and participate in his or her inner experience.

As you might imagine, this exercise can become very intense. Not everyone is a suitable partner. Select as a partner someone who can maintain the necessary mix of curiosity and objectivity. During the exercise, both of you will be dealing with subtle displays of emotion, often so subtle that you can't be certain of the accuracy of your readings. But in contrast to ordinary social exchanges, you will have an opportunity a few moments later to test the accuracy of your emotional perceptiveness when the other person tells you what he or she was thinking and feeling. And you will have the chance to observe and contrast the subtle facial expressions that accompany emotions like sadness and happiness.

While this exercise has a good deal of subjectivity to it—some people observe no change in their partner's appearance—it is based on sound neurological principles. Starting with Charles Darwin's 1872 book *The Expression of the Emotions in Man and Animals*, scientists have known that each emotion carries with it a distinct facial expression. In the ensuing 129 years, neuroscientists have learned the brain mechanism involved in emotional expression. We both express our own emotions and read the emotions of others primarily through the activity of the right hemisphere.

The first hint of this right-hemisphere specialization for emotion came from observations of some patients suffering from brain diseases affecting the right hemisphere. These patients cannot distinguish, say, an angry expression from a bored one. A similar incapacity exists among some autistic people who overinterpret or misinterpret others' emotions or facial expressions. Whatever the cause of this loss of emotional interpretive ability, it is exceedingly disabling since success in life depends a great deal upon the ability to read the emotional responses of other people and control, at least to some extent, the outer expressions of one's own feelings. Some of us are more skilled at this than others (in a significant number of cases, the right hemispheres of women show enhanced sensitivity, more so than in men; women also do better at concealing emotions if circumstances call for such dissimulation). But wherever you stand on this spectrum, an exercise like the one described above can enhance your ability to perceive the emotional expressions of others. The exercise will help you and your partner to connect with your own emotional experiences. This integrating experience will help you develop your ability not only to remember events and people from your past, but also to integrate them with your emotional experiences at that time.

Of all our senses, smell provides the surest means of enhancing emotional memory. We have Marcel Proust to thank for this insight. He discovered quite by accident that he could emotionally relive past experiences after tasting and smelling a certain small, shell-shaped cake called a madeleine. The intensity of the emotions aroused by his experience suggested to him that the senses provide the surest way of recapturing memories of the past. (*The Past Recaptured* is the title of one of the volumes in his epic work, *Remembrance of Things Past*.)

Although Proust knew little about the brain, he intuitively arrived at an insight later achieved by neuroscientists about the intimate interrelationship between taste and smell (the components of flavor) and memory. Smell is so emotionally evocative because the olfactory nerve is the only sensory channel that links directly to the brain's emotional centers in the limbic system. All of the other senses reach the limbic system through intermediary connections. This explains why perfumes and other scents can arouse strong emotional feelings. So if you want to enhance your emotional memory, you should start working with scents and smells. Here is another exercise described to me by my daughter Jennifer.

Ask three or four of your friends to bring with them to your house or apartment three of their favorite smells. These can range from perfumes and aftershaves to such things as newly mowed grass, candies, leather bags, freshly baked cookies, sandalwood, a flower, crayons, and the like. The important requirement is that the smell must be pleasing to the person bringing it.

With all of the items lined up on a table, each person walks along the table sampling the aromas. When this is concluded, everyone tells the others what scent he or she liked the best and why. Most important, everyone should describe what memories the scents evoked and rate the intensity of the ensuing feeling accompanying that memory on a scale ranging from a low of 1 (not very emotionally intense at all) to 10 (very intense and very arousing). Finally, each person should strive to come up with a specific, emotionally charged incident from the past associated with his or her selected scent. With the recovery of that memory, the person should talk or write about what he or she recalls of his or her feelings at the time.

One final exercise in the evocation of emotional memory: Find a picture of yourself taken when you were one-half your present age. For instance, when Jennifer showed me this exercise she was twenty-eight, and she selected a picture of herself taken when she was fourteen. After staring at the picture for several minutes, she started writing a letter from her fourteen-year-old self to her twenty-eight-year-old self. She didn't pause, but kept writing all of the concerns about her future that she had felt when fourteen. Where would she go to school? What would she select as a career? Where would she be living? Would she be married? Where and with whom would she spend New Year's Eve 2000? As the exercise progressed, the writing flowed more easily and took on its own steady rhythm. In the second part of the exercise, she responded to the letter from her present vantage point as a twenty-eight-year-old: "You will attend college at Georgetown and although at 28 you still won't be married the absence of a husband won't bother you the way you thought that it would in your letter to me at 14 years of age. Now at 28 so many things are important to me that don't occur to you at 14."

The goal of this exercise, as with the ones suggested earlier, is for you to relive not just the memory of an experience, but the emotions that accompanied that experience. If you are successful, you will uncover memories of experiences you haven't thought about in years. For instance, the smell of newly mowed grass elicited in one participant a vivid memory of playing in the yard with her sisters as a young child.

As a final step in the development of emotional memory, you might want to create some exercises of your own. To help you with that goal, I suggest you read Konstantin Stanislavsky's *An Actor Prepares*. It is a storehouse of techniques for not only remembering but also reliving moments from your past.

9

Think in terms of brain geography.

*A*reas of the brain are specialized for different functions. Reading activates your occipital and frontal brain areas. Listening to music with your eyes closed fires up your temporal, frontal, and cerebellar areas. Think of this specialization in geographic terms and combat mental fatigue by using principles of brain operation based on cerebral geography. As a starter, learn about the specialized functions of the two cerebral hemispheres.

In the 1970s, the notion took hold in the popular culture that everybody was either "right" or "left" brained. This concept evolved from a misunderstanding of the work of Nobel Prize–winning neuroscientist Roger Sperry and his associates.

Sperry based his concepts of hemisphere specialization on his experimental findings in epileptics who had undergone an operation for relief of the condition. The operation consisted of cutting the corpus callosum, the bundle of nerve fibers that normally unites the two hemispheres. As a result of the operation, epileptic discharges remained confined to one cerebral hemisphere rather than spreading across the corpus callosum to the other hemisphere and thereby causing a generalized epileptic seizure.

During his research with these "split-brain" patients (as they were referred to), Sperry discovered that each of the hemispheres operated independently from the other and each carried out specialized functions. Figure C, on page 24, illustrates some of the specialized functions of each hemisphere.

To appreciate these differences, look up from this book and see what is around you. When I look out into the woods where autumn leaves are falling from the trees, my recognition of the pattern and form of the trees before me involves synthesis and parallel processing: I see many different aspects of the woods at once. The right hemisphere is specialized for mediating these features. But the verbal description I just gave (leaves falling from trees) analyzed the woods and selected for description only one of its innumerable features. This required the use of the left hemisphere, which deals with words and language (both spoken and written). The left hemisphere tends to break things into their component parts, and it attends to distinguishing rather than common features. It processes the world in a linear, sequential manner.

In contrast, the right hemisphere relies less on words and language; it's better at perceiving the "whole picture" by synthesizing and attending to general configurations. It engages in parallel processing, which involves many operations going on at the same time.

In my example, each hemisphere, though responding to different features of the woods, is acting simultaneously and in intimate collaboration with the other. While I observe the woods outside my window in its totality, I also attend to different features according to my purpose. Am I writing a poem about autumn, or merely assessing whether or not rain seems likely? As one brain researcher put it, the brain is always "purposive" and employs whatever areas are most appropriate for the task at hand. Thus, it doesn't make sense to speak of a person as if he or she is operating with only one hemisphere. For this reason, Sperry's findings on the "split-brain" patients are of only limited application to the rest of us. That's because in contrast to

Sperry's patients, we retain normal nerve fiber connections uniting our two hemispheres. In other words, our brain functions as a unity. Nonetheless, knowing about the specialization patterns of the two hemispheres can provide useful strategies to enhance our brain's overall performance.

By keeping in mind the specialization patterns of the two hemispheres, you can learn to think of the brain in geographical terms. What do I mean by that? Like the geography we studied in grade school, cerebral geography deals with location and position. But instead of dealing with the earth's surface, cerebral geography deals with the brain. As an elementary principle, the brain operates most efficiently when different rather than similar areas are activated simultaneously. When the same area is called upon to do two different things, an "interference effect" is produced. Therefore, try to avoid doing two things at once that activate the same parts of the brain. Think back to the frustration you often experience when someone tries to get you to do too many things at once. "I have only two hands!" you announce with some impatience. But it's not the absence of more than two hands that's usually the problem. Rather, your frustration arises from two competing demands that use the same brain areas. For example, consider two variations of the following scenario.

You're sitting at your desk engaged in an important telephone conversation. Your assistant enters, stands in front of your desk, and nervously starts to spill out to you in several sentences an equally important and somewhat complicated piece of information. If you're like most people, you will experience difficulty splitting your attention. If you listen to your assistant, you'll lose the thread of the phone conversation. But if you don't shift some attention from the phone conversation, you'll have no idea what your assistant is trying to tell you. You find such a situation stressful because your brain is balking at the need to operate less efficiently in the face of two competing tasks carried out by the same areas.

In a variation of this imagined scenario, everything else remains the same with one exception: Instead of verbally communicating the information, your assistant slips a note in front of you that contains the same information. Which situation would you find easier to deal with?

Most people would prefer receiving the written note because it creates less conflict. Listening to the phone conversation while reading your secretary's note involves two different areas in the left hemisphere. But listening simultaneously to the person on the phone and your secretary talking on different subjects utilizes the same areas, or, to use a computer analogy, ties up the same circuits.

A similar conflict is responsible for the difficulty you encounter at a cocktail party when you try to monitor an adjoining conversation while simultaneously trying to keep up your end of a face-to-face conversation. You experience a sense of internal strain. And if you try to monitor yet a third conversation by listening to another nearby couple, the strain gets even worse because you're stretching your brain's capacity to the limit, according to researchers. Remember this general rule: You will experience difficulty whenever you simultaneously carry out two similar language-based activities. But you can reduce the difficulty by varying the situation so that you're using different parts of your brain, such as listening to one communication while reading another, instead of trying to listen to two different conversations at once.

Another example: reading or writing can be comfortably combined with listening to music, since two different hemispheres are involved (except in musicians, who tend to use the left hemisphere for both language and music). But conflict will result if you're attentively listening to the words of, say, an opera while reading a thought-provoking book. Since you're concentrating on the words of the opera, you're using the language areas instead the musical appreciation areas. The two activities will conflict with each other and you're likely to feel fatigued or strained.

I'm not claiming, incidentally, that such interference effects can't be overcome. But you do create more difficulty for yourself when you work in opposition to the brain's natural processing. Can that processing be changed? I believe it can. No two brains are exactly the same and people vary considerably when it comes to what they con-sider sensory overload. In addition, life experience and conditioning are important.

For instance, the brain circuitry of today's high school and college students represents the culmination of a lifelong exposure to tech-nologically mediated sensory stimulation. In many instances, these young people can comfortably manage a frequency and intensity of stimulation that earlier, less technologically inclined generations would experience as sensory "flooding," or sensory overload. So I'm not suggesting that everyone will experience interference effects. Depending on your age and exposure to multitasking, you may be able to function just fine under conditions of sensory overload. Instead, I'm trying to provide you with some rules that will help your brain function optimally. Think in terms of cerebral geography. Consult Figure C, on page 24, to review what each hemisphere does best and avoid challenging the same brain area at the same time.

As a practical application of your new knowledge of cerebral geography, look for ways of combating mental fatigue by switching to activities that use different parts of the brain.

If you're engaged in a task that involves reading or writing, take a brain break by switching to something that involves patterns or forms. Look up from your work and mentally engage in a *feng shui* exercise. In your imagination, rearrange the furnishings and acces-sories in the room. To do this, you don't have to believe that this ancient Chinese practice will guarantee your success or change your fortune. For even if you don't buy into these beliefs, you will experi-ence a lessening from the sense of mental fatigue.

As an alternative, you might page through a magazine dedicated to architecture, fashion, or design. You choose. But whatever your choice, just keep in mind that your purpose is to use parts of your brain unrelated to speech and writing. As you make the switch from language to form and pattern processing, a PET scan of your brain taken at the time would show a shift in brain activity. The verbal areas will "power down" to a restful state, while the holistic processing areas (primarily in the right hemisphere) will glow bright red or orange, an indicator of increased glucose consumption.

One of my methods for balancing the brain is to shift back and forth between two favorite one-person games. The left hemisphere game is Crossword Dice. This consists of seven dice with letters rather than numbers on the six faces. After tossing all seven dice, you have one minute to create as many words as you can by arranging the dice. The game provides a nice mix of the best aspects of a crossword puzzle and a game of Scrabble.

The second game, Set, challenges the right hemisphere. A product of the inventive mind of Marsha Fulco, Set consists of two decks of cards. In this game of visual perception, each card has four varying features: number, symbol, shading, and color. For instance, a card may show one shaded green triangle. A second card may display two clear red triangles. The goal is to rapidly select from a random deal of twelve cards arranged in three rows of four a "set" of three cards in which each feature is *either* the same on each card *or* different on each card. In other words, each of the four features in the set of three cards is either *common* to all three cards or *different* on each card.

Finally, if I'm in need of an exercise that supercharges the form-manipulating powers of my nonverbal right hemisphere, I play a round of the game Rush Hour. This game consists of a number of cars and trucks set out on a grid. Many of the vehicles block the advance of others. It's not quite total gridlock, but it's close. The purpose of the game is to move the blocking cars and trucks up or down, left or right, until a path is cleared for one red car to exit through the single opening in the grid frame. No vehicles can be lifted; they must be skillfully moved along the grid frame. After many hours of playing this challenging game designed by the game inventors at Binary Arts in Alexandria, Virginia, I can personally attest that the game provides a real challenge of your powers of concentration, patience, visualization, and form recognition.

Together, these games provide the brain equivalent of shifting from, say, an endurance activity like long-distance jogging to a slow-motion activity like tai chi. Just as these different physical exercises emphasize different muscles and movement patterns, Crossword Dice, Set, and Rush Hour challenge different brain areas; as a consequence, mental fatigue just melts away. Try these games yourself.

If you want to foster personal creativity, channel your efforts along lines that take full advantage of your brain's organization and optimal functioning.

Here's another brain-based method of boosting creativity by shifting attention from one hemisphere to the other. Attend to the thoughts (left) and images (right) that occur just prior to falling asleep and during the first few moments upon awakening. At such times, you'll be less distracted and inhibited by external activities and your response to them, and thus more open to new and original insights. Keep a small tape recorder by your bedside and dictate the contents of a dream before it's forgotten. Even put down those thoughts that interfere with getting to sleep. What new or unusual ideas occur? What scenarios do you tend to play over and over in your mind? In the morning, you can transfer some of this material into your notebook.

All of these exercises serve the common purpose of breaking down artificial barriers that you've set up that interfere with the brain's performance. By practicing them, you can unify seemingly diverse areas of functioning and thus enhance your brain's efficiency and level of performance.

To return to my original example of looking out at the woods, the richer my knowledge of the flora and fauna of the woods (a left-hemisphere process), the more I'll be able to see. This holds true even if I don't consciously access the features that distinguish, say, the leaves of the elm from those of the oak. Our perceptions take on richness and depth as a result of all the things that we learn. The eye is not a camera that objectively takes a photo of the "world out there." Rather, what the eye sees is determined by what the brain has learned. This suggests a short mantra: learn more, see more. For instance, when I encounter a person on the street with an unusual gait, my neurological training helps me to figure out whether they may be suffering from a brain disease, an orthopedic dysfunction, or simply from what John Cleese used to refer to as "funny walks." In contrast, when encountering the same person, my friend Frank Wright, an artist, would most likely concentrate not on the person's gait but on his or her facial features and an estimation of what kind of portrait subject the person might make. But both neurologist and artist will perceive the person as a whole: the result of the integrated action of the two hemispheres.

10

Develop linkages associating as many things as you can.

$\mathcal{D}$on't force a synthesis. Your brain will take care of that automatically. But you can help that synthetic process by keeping a handwritten journal or, if you're using a computer, a file containing your thoughts and associations. Put aside an afternoon each month and page or scroll through your entries. While doing this, write out in your journal or type into your computer your comments about the relationships that occur to you about earlier events and link them to current ideas and concerns. If you come up empty, here is an exercise you can carry out using a large artist's sketchbook (I use an 11″ × 14″ archival-quality pad that can be bought in any art-supply store).

Open the book so that two blank pages face each other across the divider. On the left-hand page, rapidly put down in words or images your ideas about a topic of current interest. (I suggest that you write no more than three or four words or phrases that can be enclosed within concentric bubbles.) On the right-hand page, explain your associations in words. For clarity, I routinely place capital letters between a linkage of one bubble with another on the left-hand page, and I use that same letter on the right-hand page where I explain my associations. The important thing is to put down within the confines of space everything that occurs to you, and to form associations linking one concept with another. When finished, this "mind map," as Tony Buzan, the originator of Mind Maps, calls it, will consist of a left-hand page of clustered associations and across from it on the right-hand page your more extended comments and associations.

Another approach to mind mapping involves a computer program called Inspiration. Instead of drawing your associations out on paper, you enter them on the screen to form an idea map. You start with the main idea in the middle of the screen. You then type in ideas associated with the main idea. These additional ideas are enclosed within symbols radiating out from the main idea. After letting the ideas flow, you then study the pattern of links between ideas in search of themes. You'll find that when you work with visual representations of ideas, you can easily discern patterns of how one idea relates to others. And when you create a visual map with Inspiration, you can recall the details better because you "see" it in your mind. The computer program incorporates all of the benefits of mind mapping by paper and pencil, along with the additional bonus of allowing you the opportunity to perpetually revise your mind map.

When preparing a mind map, don't inhibit yourself by self-criticism. Start writing and keep linking and associating for fifteen minutes. Your aim in this linking exercise is to increase your critical and observational powers, enhance your pattern recognition, bolster your synthetic and creative skills, and improve your ability to communicate in ways that will be comprehensible to others. Best of all, you can begin anywhere in the chain of associations created by your brain. As nineteenth-century psychologist William James described the process, "Start from any idea whatever, and the entire range of your ideas is potentially at your disposal. . . . The entire potential content of one's consciousness is accessible from any one of its points."

As James also pointed out, we can only work the law of association backward. That is, by starting from one node in our current web of associations, we can never decipher in advance just what we will be thinking five minutes later. It's as difficult as predicting the exact patterning and sequence of individual neurons interacting with one another within the brain. But you can always work the pattern of associations backward, starting with your current thoughts. This enhances memory, shores up connections, and, equally important, often provides insights and surprises. Here is an exercise that sharpens your ability in tracking your associations.

Purchase or borrow a digital watch with a timed alarm function. Have someone else set the alarm to go off at a time unknown to you several hours in the future when you're likely to be awake and not overwhelmed with work or domestic demands. At the instant the alarm sounds, take careful note of your thoughts and feelings. Try to recall the thought immediately preceding the alarm, and then the thought before that one, and then the thought leading up to that thought, and so on. Track the linkages as far back as you can. Don't guess and don't make anything up. At first, you probably won't be able to trace the contents of your consciousness more than a few steps. But with practice, you will be able to track back over a dozen or more associations.

Another variation of the association exercise is to apply it to a conversation. With practice, you can get as good as psychiatrists and novelists at tracking conversational patterns and reconstructing dialogues. Use a tape recorder to record five or ten minutes of casual conversation with a friend. Later, try to reconstruct the conversation in your mind as precisely as possible. When you can't come up with anything else, listen to the tape of the original conversation and compare it to your recollections. Since you were a participant in the dialogue, its reconstruction should come more easily than with recorded conversations in which you did not participate.

After some practice, you should be able to track your thought patterns as well as reconstruct your own and other people's conversations from memory. When you become skilled at this, you'll notice the repetition of certain ideas and "themes." List them and free-associate some possible explanations. When reviewing your recollections of conversations, try to figure out how and why certain topics arose. In doing so, you'll discover that most conversations aren't nearly as casual, spontaneous, and undirected as they initially seem. Try to identify the themes as they emerge. Why did a particular topic come up at *this* point in the conversation? Why do your own thoughts keep returning to *that* specific subject? Use the material you've gained from your observations. Don't force an explanation when one doesn't emerge naturally. It isn't always possible to reach a conclusion, and you should remain aware of the deeply subjective nature of the thought-tracking process. Instead of certainties, you're in search of possibilities. Above all, don't draw fixed conclusions (particularly negative ones) on the basis of your analyses.

In a discussion with a psychoanalyst friend, I learned that thought tracking—or "self-analysis," as the psychoanalysts refer to it—has a long but generally little-known history in psychoanalysis. Self-analysis was, of course, the method used by Freud. It provided him the insights that led to the development of psychoanalysis. Today, psychoanalysts rely upon self-analysis during the years following their formal analysis. They train themselves to remain acutely aware of the stream and content of their own thoughts while simultaneously paying careful attention to the associations that arise during their conversations with others. You can do the same and with equal benefit. Here is the method I've adopted from psychoanalyst Theodore Reik.

Speak into a small, inconspicuous tape recorder all the thoughts that occur to you over fifteen minutes. This offers several advantages over writing in a diary or journal. "The road from thought to speech is shorter than from thinking to writing," according to Reik. "What we think is only what we say within ourselves without pronouncing the words. In addition spoken words have an emotional quality different from the words that have only been thought." Thus, a tape recorder provides the additional advantage of allowing one to hear oneself think.

Another method of thought tracking involves writing down all of the associations that occur to you in response to two seemingly unrelated events, topics, or objects. As an example, here are the linkages produced by my thoughts over a fifteen-minute period after looking through a magazine and selecting at random two pictures taken from advertisements of seemingly unrelated objects. One is a picture of sunglasses, the other a tube of lipstick:

Sunglasses were developed to shield the eyes from the harmful effects of the sun while lipstick protects the lips from dryness, a by-product of exposure to the sun. Both products resulted from advances in synthetic chemistry, specifically the synthesis of polymers. But synthetic chemistry also created polystyrenes and aerosols, the chemicals found in deodorants and shaving creams. Increase in the use of these products is depleting the ozone layer and, as a by-product, increasing the incidence of cataract disease and lip cancer secondary to sun exposure. But polystyrenes also made possible the development of the photographic film that captured the images of the sunglasses and lipstick that I'm studying in the magazine. Sunglasses lend to their wearer an element of interest, mystery, or glamour (Jackie Kennedy), which increases the appeal of sunglasses and, as an unintentional by-product, induces increasing numbers of people to wear the glasses and thus cut down their chances of contracting sun-related cancers. But sunglasses are also sinister (Mafia dons are invariably depicted in sunglasses; Idi Amin wore reflective sunglasses so that his victims could only see their terrified expressions reflected back at them). Amin and the Mafia are associated with death, and their dark glasses or "shades" suggest the inhabitants of Hades. Used in the singular, a "shade" is a visor for shielding the eyes from strong light and, hence, a forerunner of "shades," a colloquial term for sunglasses. But a shade is also a scientific apparatus or shutter for intercepting light passing through the camera that enabled the photographer to take the pictures before me of the tube of lipstick and the sunglasses.

Pick two items at random and try the associative method your-self. Aim for what Glass Bead Game expert Chris Severud suggests: ". . . the composition and presentation of a connected system of diverse facts, concepts and ideas." Severud is a teacher and devel-oper of games aimed at synthesizing "the relationships between dif-ferent disciplines, with the main focus on depicting the 'threads' that connect them."

No two individuals will form the same patterns because no two indi-viduals possess identical brains or have undergone identical experi-ences. My own associations in the sunglasses-lipstick example were no doubt heavily influenced by my scientific and medical education. If your background is in the humanities, polystyrenes, ozone layers, and cancers aren't likely to be among the first associations that spring to mind. More likely, your patterns will evolve on the basis of your expe-rience.

"Simple patterns are connected to form increasingly sophisticated and complex patterns," according to Severud, who suggests that our goal involves "perceiving, creating, and making these patterns 'our own.'"

An interesting and challenging variation of this technique of weaving increasingly complex patterns of ideas involves taking an historical event and quickly listing its consequences. For example, Argentine writer Jorge Luis Borges listed the following consequences of importing black slaves to America:

Handy's blues, the success in Paris of the Uruguayan painter Dr. Pedro Figari, the fine rough prose of the equally Uruguayan Vicente Rossi, the mythological stature of Abraham Lincoln, the five hun-dred thousand dead of the American Civil War, the thirty-three hundred spent on military pensions, the stature of the imaginary black soldier Falucho, the inclusion of the verb "to lynch" in the thirteenth edition of *The Dictionary of the Spanish Academy of Let-ters,* the impetuous film *Hallelujah,* the sturdy bayonet charge of Soler at the head of the black regiment at the Battle of Cerrito, the charm of Miss So-and So, the black man who killed Martin Fierro, the deplorable rumba *The Peanut Vendor,* the arrested and jailed napoleonist Toussaint L'Ouverture, the cross and the serpent in Haiti, the blood of the goats beheaded by the *papaloi's* machete, the *habanera,* mother of the tango, the *candomblé.*

While many of Borges's references are now obscure and largely unknown to anyone lacking his extraordinary erudition, others are easily recognizable. But to Borges, such a complex intellectual tapestry naturally flowed from the interconnections created by his many years of study. While most of us can't expect to come up with such a rich series of associations, we can enhance our brain's performance and our creativity by expanding our neuronal networks and trying to see how well we can do.

These different exercises will also provide you with a personal demonstration of how your brain works. In addition, they will enhance your powers of observation, improve your memory, help you discover linkages between past and present, and heighten your alertness and awareness. Observe that your associations aren't logical or linear, but more like the pinball process described in chapter 2 by James Burke. As we discussed in chapter 3, the brain is a weaver of elaborate and complicated montages.

At this point, stop reading and try one of the methods suggested in this chapter. If you haven't done this kind of thing before, I'd recommend the picture method as an introduction to the technique. Cut out and place two unrelated pictures beside each other and look at them for about ten to fifteen seconds. Then write down or dictate into a recorder as many linkages as possible based on your brain's thread of connected facts, concepts, and ideas. But whatever the association method you may choose, you will be amply rewarded by the insights it will provide.

11

Engage in activities that stimulate extensive portions of the brain.

To accomplish this goal, start working on your powers of concentration. Via a series of simple tests, neuroscientists discovered the power of concentration to be a whole-brain exercise. A volunteer slipped her head inside a PET scanner while placing her writing hand on the keypad of a small laptop computer. Proceeding by trial and error, she tried to figure out an unknown sequence of finger taps selected by the experimenters. A record of the accuracy of her performance was displayed on a small monitor in front of her. Whenever she selected a correct key in the sequence a signal would appear on the screen. After she came up with the total sequence, the experimenters urged her to keep tapping it out in an automatic rhythmic pattern. After an hour, she could traipse through the pattern without thinking about it at all.

In the experiment, the subject's PET pattern changed within moments of her figuring out the sequence. During the early effortful period of the experiment prior to her learning the sequence, PET scan activation occurred over extensive areas of her brain. This included higher cognitive areas like the prefrontal lobes, involved in planning and working the memory; the basal ganglia, responsible for unconscious automated motor movements; and the cerebellum, that orchestrator of smooth coordination. But the moment she learned the pattern, only those parts of the motor cortex involved in the finger movements displayed activation.

To an observer unacquainted with the experiment, the subject's performance looked the same throughout: a person lying in a scanner while tapping out a series of keystrokes. But such a superficial observation would, of course, ignore the important brain changes that occurred as the experiment progressed. Initially, the subject had to concentrate in order to figure out the correct sequence. But after she learned the sequence and practiced it awhile, she could turn her attention elsewhere and even daydream. A similar change in brain activity takes place when a novice driver gains road experience. With sufficient practice, he or she can think about all sorts of other things while driving.

Similar brain changes occur during the course of any mental effort. In a test carried out at Washington University in St. Louis, volunteers inside the PET scan try to come up with verbs to match a series of nouns. For instance, *kitchen* evokes in some volunteers the words *cook* or *clean*. This generation of verbs activates widespread areas of the brain, including the left frontal cortex, the left temporal cortex, the anterior cingulate cortex, and the right cerebellar cortex.

But dramatically different PET results emerge if the volunteers are given the opportunity to practice the word-generation task before entering the PET scanner. In this case, the results are similar to the pattern evoked by merely reading the words from a prepared list.

Practice, of course, decreases the need for concentration. It also has the unfortunate effect of turning off large portions of the brain. Thus, if you become too wedded to routine, you're turning off important brain areas and interfering with your brain's optimal performance. But you can reverse this process by transforming routine activities into challenges. When you do, those important brain areas are recruited once again. This is important because these widely dispersed brain areas form a coherent system involving a great number of neuronal networks.

In practical terms, the Washington University research provides experimental support for the benefits of striving for new challenges in your work and career. It's literally brain- and mind-numbing to work at unchallenging, repetitive jobs. Repetitions of the same dull routines exact a high price: functional atrophy of large portions of the brain. But, on occasion, even the most challenging job has its downtime. The last part of the finger-tapping experiments suggests an antidote for you whenever you're in a rut, or experiencing downtime fatigue.

After the volunteers had become accustomed to their word-generation task (and turning off portions of their brains in the process), the experimenter asked them to pay renewed attention to the now automated finger-tapping sequence. When they did this, the prefrontal cortex, along with the other distributed networks, became active once again.

So if you're momentarily forced to engage in repetitive, "mindless" activities, concentrate on them, enter fully into what you're doing—perhaps come up with some little variation—and your brain will kick back into concerted action.

One caveat: Sometimes during the regular repetition of certain activities you're better off allowing your subcortex to take control. For instance, unless you're training to become a Grand Prix driver, you're probably better off not paying too much conscious attention to your driving habits; instead, under most road conditions, trust the automated driving script embedded over the years within your subcortex. (That's assuming, of course, that the script involves safe and courteous driving habits; if it doesn't, then driver retraining will not only improve your driving habits but provide a socializing as well as a brain-enhancing experience.)

The finger-tapping and language experiments suggest that large areas of the brain can be recruited into action whenever we concentrate fully on whatever we're doing at the moment. Conscious attention renders the most routine task novel once again. Remember: The brain thrives on novelty. Strive to transform even the most routine tasks into novel and challenging endeavors.

12

Let the brain just be the brain.

To allow your brain to operate at its best, it is first necessary to gain control over the factors that interfere with its optimal functioning. Although the influence of these factors may vary from person to person, they include:

- Difficulties in concentration and focus
- Poor imaging ability
- Memory weaknesses
- Organizational problems
- Mood disorders
- Performance anxiety
- Lack of follow-through
- Ignorance of the brain's machinery

The steps in the following chapters aim at removing the most common impediments to enhanced brain function. First, your brain works best when you don't try to micromanage it by too much conscious direction. You also must free it from the impediments imposed by unregulated emotions and the harmful effects of stress.

Despite popular notions to the contrary, the brain does not operate like a computer or any other machine. That's why we have to stop forcing it to act in ways that are unnatural and unproductive. For example, some very bright students do poorly on standardized tests because when answering questions they insist on engaging in "self-talk" about the correct answer instead of simply reading the question and picking the answer that seems correct to them.

Insightful teachers deliver a similar message to their students at test time: don't think too much about the question; just choose the answer that seems correct and move on to the next question. This is not a recommendation for wild guessing, incidentally. If the student has prepared for the test and knows the subject, his or her brain will pick out the correct answer without recourse to any inner dialogue. This natural ability to immediately discern the correct response forms the basis for many instances of intuition; the brain knows and selects the correct answer.

Nor is this anxiety about getting things "right," and thus skewing the brain's natural powers, confined to the classroom. I first became aware of this process a few years ago when I took my twelve-year-old daughter Ann for an eye exam. Toward the end of the exam, the ophthalmologist asked her to look through several lenses presented one at a time and decide which lens provided the clearest image of letters flashed on a screen. This was the final stage of her eye exam, a fine-tuning aimed at determining the best possible lenses for my daughter's glasses. Since the distinctions between the lenses involved subtle differences, she was requested to "simply look and tell me which lens looks clearer to you." But instead of simply looking at the letters and immediately reporting on the clarity provided by the different lenses, she hesitated in order to, as she told the doctor, "think it over for a second."

"Don't think. Just look and immediately report what you see. In

this part of the exam first answers are always best answers," the ophthalmologist told Ann. He then briefly elaborated that in such a situation "thinking" has no role to play. Her best bet was to simply
"look and choose, look and choose."

My daughter's anxiety about making a mistake and thus ending up
with the "wrong" lenses temporarily disrupted the natural and spontaneous cooperation between eye and brain. Her request for the opportunity to stop and "think" resulted from an overreliance on putting
everything into words and attempting to reason out what should have
been nothing more than reporting on a simple sense perception.

The art critic Max Friedlander made a similar point when com-
menting on how an expert identifies the work of a specific artist: "Correct attributions generally appear spontaneously and 'prima vista.' We
recognize a friend without ever having determined wherein his particular qualities lie and that with a certainty that not even the most
detailed description can give."

Balancing the efforts of the two hemispheres and thus enhancing
mental endurance can also be done via physical exercises. But the
exercises must emphasize balance and coordination and thereby
involve the cerebellum. As an example, try the following exercise.
Best of all, try it at the conclusion of some strenuous mental exercise,
perhaps at the end of a challenging day at the office.

Hold a tennis ball in your nondominant hand (the left hand for
right-handers). Now, while looking straight ahead, sweep your hand
upward and toss the ball in an arc across to your dominant hand.
Make sure that the ball ascends high enough to prevent your observing its progress. Did you catch it?

Most people will fail this test unless they're involved in some regular activity that demands awareness of the position of their body in
the space around them (as are dancers and athletes). If you failed on
the first try, consider your failure a deserved payback for all those
hours in the office spent thinking, writing, and talking. Such one-
sidedness in your activities exacts a toll. For one thing, your brain's
operations will be skewed toward the overuse of introspection and

inner speech ("Now, the best way of catching this ball would be to . . ."). All of us are engaged in carrying out such silent conversations with ourselves, which cognitive psychologists refer to as "self-talk." But not all activities benefit from self-talk. When performing the ball-catching exercise, having an inner dialogue with yourself is the wrong way to proceed. Don't think about it: "Just do it," as the Nike advertisements put it. In fact, most exercises are best performed without recourse to any kind of inner speech. It shifts the balance toward left-hemisphere language processing, which is a disadvantage when doing something that relies on form, pace, or movement perception.

If you didn't catch the ball, try a simpler exercise. Stand in front of a mirror with your raised hands palms-upward. Hold the tennis ball in one of your hands. Look into the mirror and see yourself holding the tennis ball in one hand with the other hand less than two feet away. Convince yourself how easy it will be to transfer the ball from one hand to the other. Then close your eyes and, without any thought or self-talk, *just do it*. Keep trying until the ball lands in the opposite hand and you successfully grasp it.

After a few attempts at this seemingly simpler exercise, most people can finally manage to catch the ball. At the moment of your first success, pay particular attention to the fleeting sensation of mixed pleasure and surprise you experience. This reflects your brain's correction for the usual imbalance between the two hemispheres created by your customary concentration on thoughts, words, and language. In this simple exercise, however, you are no longer operating via words and concepts but according to a refreshing and relaxing appreciation of your body in space.

Any number of activities can shift the balance to the body-brain and away from the inner talk of the mind-brain. That's why driving can be fun, but also more treacherous when daydreaming—that is, attending to the inner reality rather than the immediate situation on the highway.

Select any activity that appeals to you in which a penalty is exacted for thinking or talking things out through inner dialogue. It can be pinball, juggling, Nintendo, or the following exercise, which can be done in the office as a fatigue fighter.

Walk about fifteen feet away from the wastepaper basket in your office. Turn your back. Then quickly turn around and toss a tennis ball (or a firmly rolled-up ball of paper) into the basket. While doing this, clear your mind of any sense of effort. With each toss, pretend that you are doing the most natural thing in the world and you are doing it fresh each time.

If you're like me, you'll find that your best shots are your early ones. As you toss more often, your performance falls off. Why? After a few tosses you figuratively (and perhaps even literally) begin talking to yourself. You begin to put too much thought and inner dialogue into the throw. As a result, you begin to miss.

A similar situation occurs with darts. It's not uncommon for a novice to beat an experienced player in the first game or so. But as the number of games increases, skill and experience win out. That's because encoded within the brain of the experienced player are neuronal networks set up during many hundreds of hours of practice. When we speak of a person's experience in any field, not just sports, we are unwittingly referring to the extent and quality of his or her brain's neuronal networks. Over several games, but not necessarily in a single game, these networks will prove superior to the trial-and-error approach of the novice.

An ill-advised strategy for getting the most out of our brain's performance is to try to force certain thoughts out of awareness. Obsessive-compulsive disorder represents an extreme example of this impulse to "control" the contents of consciousness for the purpose of getting things "right." In my professional practice of neuropsychiatry, I frequently encounter men and women who try to force themselves to stop thinking about such things as whether they may have left their front door unlocked. (They've never failed to lock their door in the past, but that knowledge isn't helpful in silencing their intrusive thoughts.)

But attempts to suppress intrusive, unwelcome thoughts aren't the exclusive domain of people with diagnosed emotional disturbances.

We all engage on occasion in what Trinity University psychologist Daniel Wegner refers to as the "white bear" phenomenon in his book *White Bears and Other Unwanted Thoughts*.

It seems that as a child, the future novelist Fyodor Dostoyevsky once challenged his little brother to stand in a corner until he could stop thinking of a white bear. Of course the child tried his hardest and, as a result, couldn't get the white bear out of his mind. In this homespun experiment, the child learned something important about the human brain: the more effort we make not to think of something, the more difficulty we experience in expelling it from our consciousnesses.

Why are we so helpless before the contents of our own mind? Professor Wegner suggests that "our difficult time with thought suppression comes when, in the sequence of conscious thoughts, we get the idea to suppress a current thought. The suppression metathought ('I'd rather not think of a white bear') is here, but the thought ('white bear') is here, too. . . . current consciousness is unable to think itself out of having a thought because this entails thinking the 'thought.'"

In other words, it's not the thought that creates the problem, but our attempt to suppress the thought. The painful mental duality created for us by our own thoughts can be countered by two measures. First, give up entirely on forcing thoughts from your mind. Accept them. Even embrace the unwanted thoughts. Allow the thoughts to occur freely, observe them, and, most important, don't fight them. Turning off the urge to suppress unwanted thoughts, it turns out, is the ultimate act of mental control.

Professor Wegner writes: "In embracing our unwanted thoughts we escape the tyranny that suppression can hold over us. We no longer must worry about our worries, no longer wish our thoughts away, no longer believe that we are plagued by images that we cannot overcome. When we turn towards those things and look at them closely they can disappear."

William James concurred: "To wrestle with a bad feeling only pins our attention on it, and keeps it still fastened in the mind: whereas, if we act as if from some better feeling, the old bad feeling soon folds its tent . . . and silently steals away."

The second remedy consists of proactively adopting positive thoughts and emotions from the people and events around you. Rather than trying to drive away distressing thoughts, try to come up with thoughts that inspire or motivate you. Think back to occasions when you performed well under conditions of stress. Seek the company of happy rather than depressed people; brighten up your living quarters; reach out toward positive and uplifting experiences, people, and things. If you take these measures, you will have at your disposal a constant supply of positive thoughts and feelings.

Despite the slightly Pollyanna-ish flavor of this second remedy, experimental psychology experiments confirm its effectiveness. Indeed, our grandmothers were giving us sound, scientifically provable advice when they spoke of the power of "positive thinking." Since the brain can only feature in the foreground one thought at a time—with all competing thoughts relegated to the background— our choice of a positive thought and our concentration on it robs the painful thought of its sting. So if you want to feel energized and capable of using your brain most effectively, free it from the hopeless task of controlling and suppressing. Let the brain operate autonomously without any attempt at controlling its operation. In this way, you will learn to take advantage of your brain's innate intuitive abilities.

13

Practice forms of mental hygiene.

In the nineteenth century, many psychiatrists and psychologists (William James among them) emphasized the importance of healthy mental attitudes and practices. They coined the term "mental hygiene" to describe the measures a person can take to make the brain function more efficiently. Just as the body benefits from exercise, good diet, and a temperate lifestyle, the brain works better if a person follows certain mental guidelines. The most important guideline involves not paying too much attention to our feelings.

"There is no better known or more generally useful precept in one's personal self-discipline, than that which bids us pay primary attention to what we do and express, and not to care too much for what we feel. Action seems to follow feeling, but really action and feeling go together; and by regulating the action, which is under the more direct control of the will, we can indirectly regulate the feeling, which is not," according to James.

Over the years, James's point of view fell out of favor. Remember the injunctions a few years ago to "let it all hang out"? And if we needed help, there was always primal scream and other therapies that emphasized getting in touch with our feelings and, most importantly, expressing them in some way, whatever the consequences for other people's sensibilities. Additional knowledge about the brain has revealed the perils of placing too much emphasis on the unrestrained expression of our emotions. Nor can we give in to negative emotional states.

For instance, people suffering from depression exhibit abnormal PET scans and other measures of brain activity. Moreover, this abnormal brain activity accompanying depression can cast a pall over events of the past. When depressed we tend to dwell on the losses and hurts we've encountered in our lives. Even good things appear paltry and inconsequential when viewed through the distorting lens created by low moods. "The self-same person, according to the line of thought he may be in, or to his emotional mood, will perceive the same impression quite differently on different occasions," wrote James.

Research shows that brain changes indicative of depression can occur in nondepressed volunteers if they allow themselves to think sad or depressing thoughts. This result suggests that, at least in the initial stages, it is the negative thoughts and attitudes that unfavorably alter brain function, rather than the other way around. In time, as the depression deepens, this sequence may be reversed; the dysfunctional brain becomes the culprit and produces increasingly depressive thoughts, ultimately culminating in illness and even suicide. But at least, in the earliest stages, this sequence can be favorably influenced by mental attitude.

One important attitude change involves keeping ourselves physically and mentally occupied. Internal distress often results from having too much empty time on our hands. Physical and mental inactivity lead to boredom, anxiety, and depression. In turn, these uncomfortable states exert powerfully negative effects on our functioning. We start to dwell on the negative, perhaps a holdover from the time when our ancestors had to contend with so many physical threats to their survival, health, and well-being.

Today most of our perceived threats don't involve death or severe physical impairment. Indeed, most of them are the creations of our own imagination. If we could learn to take our situations and ourselves less seriously, we would be better able to cope. To be sure, some of life's more serious threats, such as the loss of a job or the breakup of a marriage, are not trivial matters. But neither do they involve life or death.

Whatever the threat, worry and other forms of negativity make things worse because they always exert a powerfully destructive effect on the brain's functioning. When worried or experiencing other negative thoughts, we find ourselves drawn toward imagined disasters. For instance, even though we may be in excellent health, we're inclined to focus on whatever minor ills may exist at the moment. At such times, our attention is exclusively focused on the threatening and the negative—whether involving other people or just us.

Since the brain can keep only one thought at a time in the foreground of consciousness, it's important to emphasize uplifting rather than depressing and negative preoccupations. While this tendency toward the morbid can be overcome by encouraging positive thinking, we can't depend entirely on pure willpower. That's why it's important to keep your brain active, challenged, and curious.

14

Turn your feelings and emotions to your advantage.

Perhaps this has happened to you: You find yourself distrusting someone but can't put into words, much less logically defend, your intuitive feelings. In the interest of remaining "reasonable" you put aside your reservations. Later, you find out to your regret that your initial hunch was correct.

Most of us have been conditioned since childhood to distrust our emotions. We are encouraged to reason things out and always be prepared to justify our decisions and actions by logic and reasoning. While such advice is not always bad, you shouldn't rely on it entirely. As discussed at the beginning of chapter 12, your brain is not a logic machine. It is organized to process emotions along with logic.

For instance, when you think back to a happy occasion in your *recent* past you don't just recall a series of "facts." You also remember the emotional significance of the event, how you "felt" at the time. A similar process occurs with hurtful or embarrassing experiences. Moreover, emotions and feelings about something or

someone occur before you've made any attempt at conscious evaluation. "Fear occurs before you know what you're afraid of," as brain
researcher Joseph LeDoux explains it. Since LeDoux's research into
emotions provides the basis for our understanding of intuition, let
me describe it in some detail.

If a rat in a cage is exposed to a sound, the animal initially orients
itself toward and pays attention to the sound, but after a few repetitions, the rat ignores it. However, the animal will respond once again
if the sound is paired with an electrical shock. After a few repetitions
of this pairing of sound and shock, the rat begins to display signs of
fear whenever it hears the sound alone. It stops what it's doing and
freezes in place. The animal's only detectable movement consists of
the rhythmic chest excursions that accompany breathing. In addition, the rat's fur stands on end, its blood pressure and heart rate
increase, and stress hormones pour into its bloodstream. In a word,
the rat is now "conditioned" so that the sound when presented alone
will elicit the fear response. This response is no different than what
occurs when the rat encounters its natural enemy, the cat.

We humans can be fear conditioned, too. If you're injured in a car
accident, it may take several months before you're completely relaxed
behind the wheel again. That's because the accident has established
within your brain a link between driving and that frightening, hurtful
experience. If the accident was a particularly serious one, you may
even experience some of the symptoms of post-traumatic stress disorder (PTSD): flashbacks of the accident, or a tendency to startle and
overreact to loud or unexpected noises. Figure I, on page 117, illustrates what's going on in your brain.

The sights and sounds and general sensory processing associated
with driving flow along established brain paths toward the thalamus, the way station and integration center for all sensory information except smell (which, as indicated in chapter 8, is channeled
directly via the olfactory nerve to all the brain's emotional centers).
From the thalamus, the sensory information proceeds along two
main pathways.

The "high road" leads from the thalamus toward the cerebral cortex, where conscious elaboration of the facts of the accident takes place. As a result, you recall the circumstances of the accident as a specific event.

But the second pathway, the "low road," also connects the thalamus with the amygdala, an emotional processing center. The amygdala is not concerned with the facts of the accident, but rather with the associated emotions. As a result of amygdalar stimulation, you reexperience, while at the wheel at a later date, the same racing of your heart and sinking feeling in your stomach that occurred seconds before the crash. If these feelings are sufficiently intense, you may not be able to drive at all.

Fortunately, the influence of the amygdala can be moderated in most instances by the cerebral cortex, where conscious elaboration of the accident takes place. We can internally talk it out and adopt a positive attitude toward the experience: "I've never had a prior accident and there's no reason to expect another. I should be glad I survived and just get on with my life."

Figure I

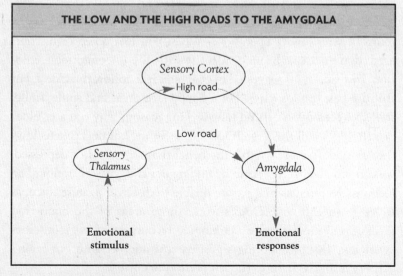

THE LOW AND THE HIGH ROADS TO THE AMYGDALA

Sensory Cortex
High road

Low road

Sensory Thalamus   *Amygdala*

Emotional stimulus   Emotional responses

Neuroscientists now understand the beneficial effects of adopting positive thoughts and attitudes about our lives and how they bring about beneficial alterations in the brain. In a PET scan study, Richard Davidson, professor of psychology and psychiatry at the University of Wisconsin-Madison, discovered that activation of the left but not the right prefrontal cortex inhibits amygdala activity and thereby dampens negative attitudes and responses.

For those of us who already have a positive outlook, it's likely our left prefrontal cortex is naturally more active than the same area in the right hemisphere. But Davidson suggests we have no reason to despair if our genes have dealt us a bad hand and our right prefrontal cortex is the more active one. Treatment with antidepressant medications can change the pattern from right-sided to left-sided activity. And for those of us who aren't excited about the prospect of taking medications, the news is also good. "I suspect that psychological treatments such as cognitive therapy will be found to produce similar effects," says Davidson. Since cognitive therapy essentially involves changing our perspectives in order to put the best face on our particular situation, it's likely a positive mental attitude may be just as effective in enhancing left prefrontal activation, thereby obviating the need for professional treatment.

Think of your negative and distressing emotional responses in terms of your brain's operations. When you feel down or discouraged, don't get caught up or identify with the uncomfortable emotion. Instead, try, as suggested in chapter 13, to follow the oldest, but still the best, philosophy: "Put a happy face on it and smile, smile, smile." At least don't spend time seeking reasons why you are "blue" or irritable. I call this search for the "meaning" of negative feelings the "Buried Treasure Myth": the belief that when sad or depressed, we can only feel better again by finding out the "reason" for our bad feelings. As often as not, we are unable to discover a cause since, as we've learned from LeDoux's work, those areas of the brain that mediate emotion operate autonomously outside of our conscious awareness. But by adopting a positive attitude, we shift our brain's activity from the right to the left prefrontal cortex.

Therefore, if you desire peak mental efficiency, take control of your feelings and emotions. Break through them by taking away their privileged mental access; consider them as no more important than the other components of your current frame of mind. Don't allow your mood to dictate your thoughts and behavior any more than you would relinquish such control to fatigue, mild hunger, or other temporary states.

In summary, your moods result from the interaction of the limbic system with the frontal and temporal lobes. When you're depressed, you tend to dwell on unfulfilling or disappointing events from your past. Even the good times seem less pleasurable when recollected during low moods. "Intellectually, I knew at the time I would feel better the next day, but I still couldn't help *feeling* at the time that my low spirits would last forever," according to one of my patients, a middle-aged writer recalling his successfully treated depression.

As my patient's statement implies, feelings can exert powerful effects on the composition of our inner landscape. But while we can't control our feelings, we are not completely at their mercy. We can use our knowledge about our brain's organization to put our feelings into perspective. So take control of your emotions.

15

Take active measures to reduce stress.

$\mathcal{E}$very one of us is caught up in a world more harried and demanding than at any time in human history. Thanks to technological advances, we have more information thrown at us in a single day than people living two centuries ago encountered over a period of several months. And we are not only exposed to a steady onslaught of information, but that information is coming at us at an increasingly frenetic pace. This creates equally frenetic forms of communication.

Growing numbers of us speak in compressed, breakneck communications aimed at getting in as much information as possible in the allotted time. If nineteenth-century conversational rhythms corresponded to the slow cadence of a horse, our rhythms are closer to a Ferrari screaming toward the finish line at a Grand Prix event. As a result of this combination of too much information coming at us too quickly, our brains are suffering from information overload. Included among the symptoms are a chronic sense of mental fatigue, an inability to distinguish the important from the trivial, impatience at being told "too much," lack of focus, difficulty concentrating, and indecisiveness stemming from a concern that available information is somehow incomplete.

But the worst aspect of stress is the physical harm that it can wreak on the brain. For instance, the brains of people suffering from an extreme form of stress known as post-traumatic stress disorder (PTSD) harbor within their hypothalamus (a collection of small but critical clusters of neurons that lies just below the thalamus) an abnormally large number of neurons that make corticotropin releasing factor (CRF). This master hormone (so called because of its wide-ranging bodily effects) then increases the release of the messenger hormone adrenocorticotropin (ACTH).

ACTH courses through the bloodstream until it reaches the adrenal glands. Upon its arrival, ACTH spurs the release from the adrenals of an important class of stress hormones called glucocorticoids. (See Figure J.) Similar outpourings of stress hormones occur in less severe, everyday forms of stress. But whether stress is overwhelming or relatively minor, it increases the number of cells making CRF.

Figure J

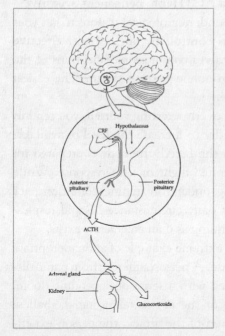

Figure J A schematic drawing of the link involving the cerebral hemispheres, the hypothalamus, and the adrenal glands. This pathway is important in mediating the stress response.

Stress produces just the opposite effect—a loss instead of a gain of cells—in another part of the brain, the hippocampus. For instance, PTSD victims, as well as monkeys subjected to experimentally administered forms of stress, lose neurons in the hippocampus, the initial encoding site for the establishment of a memory.

Indeed, if sufficient hippocampal cells die off, this vitally important brain structure actually shrinks in size. Both PTSD and severe depression can lead to cell loss and resulting hippocampal atrophy. And the greater the stress, the greater the hippocampal atrophy, as suggested from a study correlating increased combat exposure among veterans and decreased hippocampal size.

What's more, today's stress can exert future repercussions. Military veterans with PTSD that resulted from their war experiences still expressed elevated CRF levels when tested a quarter of a century later! And when adults who had been abused as children experience stress, their ACTH overreacts, suggesting that their early life traumas have forced both CRH and ACTH into permanent overdrive.

In short, there are a lot of sound, neurological reasons to get your stress response under optimum control. By far the most effective method for reducing stress involves conscious modifications of the processes controlled by the autonomic nervous system. The easiest to modify is your breathing rate.

Whenever you're excited or overly exerting yourself, you tend to breathe deeper and faster in order to increase the level of available oxygen. With more oxygen in the blood, the body is prepared for emergency situations, the so-called flight or fight response. While this response can be lifesaving under threatening conditions, it's extremely harmful under most daily circumstances. Rapid respiration tricks the brain into responding as if an emergency exists.

Panic disorder represents an extreme example of an inappropriate flight or fight respiratory response. A person suffering from panic disorder suddenly becomes afflicted with a sense of impending doom. In response to this feeling, he or she begins taking rapid, shallow breaths. With further progression of the attack, the person experiences a sensation of restricted or compromised breathing. This misperception provokes the person into breathing even harder and faster. Eventually, this combination of a subjective sense of suffocation and the ensuing efforts to combat the sensation via compensatory overbreathing leads to an escalation of the panic and in many instances flight to the nearest emergency room.

When seen by the doctor, the panicked patient is caught up in a vicious cycle: his fear-induced rapid breathing is bringing about an imbalance of oxygen and carbon dioxide in the blood. This imbalance leads to more panic and, in compensation, even more rapid breathing. While sedative medications can be depended upon to break the panic, a similar result can often be achieved simply by getting the person to breathe more slowly. In this case, a change in the sufferer's mental attitude plays the major role in bringing about positive change.

Of course, panic disorder is just that: *a disorder*. Most of us don't experience such extremes of stress-related anxiety. Nor do the same things prove equally stressful to different people. "One person's stress is another person's challenge," as one insightful observer put it.

What situation or activity would you identify as the most stressful for you? Surprisingly, public speaking heads the list of activities rated as stressful by the majority of Americans. In fact, on a list of stressful experiences, public speaking ranks higher than death! "Public speaking is the epitome of social stressors," according to Huda Akil, a scientist at the University of Michigan's Mental Health Research Institute.

But whatever you find most stressful, Akil's research on stress has important implications for you. She discovered that the greatest stress for animals occurs when they are placed in a position over which they can exert little control. For instance, an animal experiences less stress when it can exert some control over an unpleasant experience like the administration of a painful, frightening electric shock to its feet. When nothing the animal tries can halt the electric shocks, the animal, deprived of even a limited sense of control, simply gives up and enters into the state of "learned helplessness."

In our own lives, learned helplessness plays an important role in stress, too. There is nothing more stressful than dreading some unpleasant experience that you have no control over. The result can be a paralyzing sense of futility, helplessness, and stress-related anxiety. The solution is to decide if you can reasonably expect to bring about a change in the situation. Certain things you will not be able to do anything about. But instead of giving in to a state of learned helplessness, change the one thing that you do retain some control over: your own attitude toward the stressful situation.

For instance, one of my migraine patients was able to decrease the frequency and severity of her headaches simply by taking a different attitude toward them. Formerly, she panicked at the first hint of an impending migraine. She would then frantically swallow several medications that often failed to stop the onset of the headache. On one occasion, she reached into the medicine cabinet and mistakenly took one of her husband's tranquilizers. Although tranquilizers aren't usually effective for migraine, they worked in her case. This suggested to me that her migraines would improve if she could learn to take a more relaxed and accepting attitude toward them. Now, instead of living in dread of another attack and reacting with panic when one begins, she stops what she's doing, sits back, closes her eyes, and says to herself: "If the headache comes it won't kill me. I have medications that will help. In the interval I'm just going to sit here and relax." Since she adopted this conscious attitude, her migraines have almost disappeared.

Perhaps the optimal approach to stress is best summed up in a prayer: "Lord, give me the strength to change the things I can change and to accept those I cannot, and the wisdom to know the difference." One way of making a difference is to pay careful attention to the pacing of our thinking and speaking.

Here are several suggestions for compensating for everyday stress created by two of the greatest culprits: "hurry sickness" and "information overload." First, work on modifying those dysfunctional breathing patterns. On pages 199–200, I detail the specific steps to take in order to use breathing control as a stress reducer. If you wish, turn to those suggestions now.

Second, slow the frenetic pace of your thinking. As an enjoyable method, I suggest you get an audio version of a favorite book and read the book while listening to the tape. *The Pickwick Papers* was a recent choice of my own. While reading through the chapters of Dickens's immortal classic of nineteenth-century English society, I listened to the reader and suppressed the instinct to jump ahead of him. Try this exercise with a favorite book of yours. This exercise will slow the pace of your reading and thinking to the rhythms intended by the author.

Of course, listening to the reading will take more time than if you turned off the audio version and silently read the book on your own. But the point of the exercise is to slow down your reading pace so as to bring it closer into line with the cadence of the spoken word. Reading and speaking weren't always so out of sync, incidentally. Before the widespread availability of the printing press, silent reading was almost unheard of, and those who could read silently were regarded with awe. Saint Augustine, speaking in the fifth century about Saint Ambrose, commented: ". . . a remarkable thing . . . when he was reading his eye glided over the pages and his heart sensed out the sense, but his voice and tongue were at rest."

Over the succeeding centuries, silent reading became the norm. While this transformation brought obvious advantages, it also resulted in people's employing different speeds and rhythms for thinking, reading, and writing. While this isn't always a bad thing (who would read an article from the sports page at the same pace as Dickens?), it can lead to stressful feelings and loss of focus. At times, thoughts come faster than the thinker can comfortably put into words. The manic patient's tortured complaint of a "racing mind" represents the extreme of this tendency.

Despite what you've heard from speed-reading advocates, that technique is only satisfactory when rapidly skimming newspapers or magazines for general information. In those instances, you care more about information and meaning than the words and style employed by the writer. Following along the printed words, while listening to the narrator reading to you via the audiotape—or, as an alternative, reading out loud to yourself—restores the natural speech rhythms intended by the author. You can "hear" the author's voice almost as if he or she were reading aloud to you. I believe this is one of the reasons for the current popularity of author readings in bookshops and elsewhere. The author speaks the words, and we hear them differently and more fully than we would reading them by ourselves at a faster pace.

Accustom yourself to reading at a slower rate and you'll gradually notice a sense of relaxation as the pace of your reading comes into sync with the audio narrator. You don't have to do this with all reading—just works of literature or other books you've selected to read for pleasure.

Rereading a favorite book provides another antidote to the stress of information overload. Writers spend years planning and writing a book, so how can you expect to get the full benefits by spending only a few hours devoted to a single reading of the work? Rereading provides the opportunity for mulling over appealing passages, concentrating on the writer's style, and adjusting your reading speed to the measured cadence of the spoken sentence. It also provides the opportunity to appreciate nuances and subtleties. You'll also discover that on many occasions your response to the book is different upon rereading.

As a third means of reducing stress and achieving peak mental performance, you must conquer or at least control performance anxiety. Public speakers, athletes, and musicians afflicted with performance anxiety "choke up" moments before a public performance. According to sports psychologists who have treated athletes and musicians for the condition, performance anxiety is usually worsened by conscious efforts to force it away. Instead, they suggest several steps that can be applied to whatever you find stressful.

First, avoid playing over negative scenarios in your mind in which all of your worst fears are realized. As Freud pointed out in 1925 in an insufficiently appreciated paper, "On Negation," the brain doesn't deal well with negatives. If you concentrate on ways of avoiding a bad outcome rather than bringing about a good one, your brain will lock onto the negative. As every tennis player knows, the surest way of coming up with a bad serve results from energy wasted on avoiding gaffes rather than concentrating on the intended ace. Concentrate on your ideas and your goals rather than focusing on the bad things that could happen, or on how nervous you're feeling.

Second, realize that practice doesn't make perfect. Only *perfect practice* makes perfect. The goal is to set up a network within the brain that can be accessed without recourse to the evaluative functions of the prefrontal cortex. Think of the motto ACT: *Analyze* what you're trying to do; *choose* from the available options; and *trust* in the value of your perfect practice.

Third, don't force concentration ("I've got to concentrate harder and get more focused"). If you try to force concentration, you've changed your goal: instead of trying to achieve a particular goal, you're now aiming at concentration—which isn't the goal, but rather a means of achieving your goal.

Finally, aim at perceptual reality. Put your experience into perspective. Continually remind yourself of your goal rather than seeking ego gratification. This shift of emphasis from inner self toward other external considerations will often lessen performance anxiety that is narcissistic in origin: Will I be acknowledged and praised? Also, remind yourself that no matter how well or poorly you do, the world isn't going to come to an end.

While it's important to think positively and avoid mental images of failure, it's also necessary to acknowledge that failure remains a possibility. But after this acknowledgment, immediately think back to a time when you performed well and transform that experience into a positive image of yourself doing well again. The goal is to replace anxiety with positive imagery and positive self-talk. If you can learn to do this, you will free your brain from the harmful effects of stress and enable it to function at its best.

16
Learn to work in concert with your personal bodily rhythms.

If your bodily rhythms correspond to the "lark," you feel at your best in the early morning hours and you do your best work within the first few hours of getting up. But as the day wears on and you approach evening your performance begins to fade. You're less able to focus, stick with tasks, and produce work of the highest quality. By bedtime, your performance is at its worst.

In contrast, if you're an "owl," you never really get started until several hours into your day. Your performance gets better as the day progresses and by early evening you may be at your most creative.

The lark and owl cycles are the basis for our everyday feelings of energy, tension, and stress. According to California State University psychologist Robert Thayer, all of us experience four basic moods every day: calm-energy, calm-tiredness, tense-energy, and tense-tiredness. The timing of these moods will vary depending on whether we are a lark or an owl.

Calm-energy is the mood we would like to experience every moment of our lives. In this state of mind we feel aroused and energetic, without any sense of fatigue or tension.

Calm-tiredness also has good feelings associated with it. Examples include that quietly fulfilled feeling that comes after a challenging and successful day at the office, or following a good meal, or after a vigorous workout. You feel tired, but calm and relaxed.

Tense-energy is that "wired" feeling, that natural "high" that comes on while you're working at peak performance and efficiency on something you're good at. While the feeling can be pleasant, even exhilarating, you certainly don't feel relaxed. Tense-energy always involves an edginess, a dynamic sense of risk that appeals to adrenaline junkies hooked on dangerous hobbies or exciting but uncertain careers.

Tense-tiredness is that totally negative mood that exists when you're overextended, stressed out, and incapable of coping. You're irritable, anxious, depressed, and generally in a "bad mood." Tense-tiredness is often accompanied by tantrums (in children and some adults), arguments, expressions of general futility, and hopelessness.

Aim to eliminate tense-tiredness while experiencing calm-energy, calm-tiredness, and tense-energy in their proper sequence. As a first step in accomplishing this, identify if you are a lark or an owl. In my own case, I'm most productive and do all of my writing within an hour of arising. At that time I feel energized, concentrated, and focused (calm-energy). I'm also intellectually aroused and excited at the prospect of writing. At the same time, I'm experiencing a delicious edginess each morning because as I start my writing, I'm facing either a blank page or computer screen (tense-energy). After several hours spent filling those pages or that computer screen—either late morning or early in the afternoon—I'm no longer in the "zone." As I stop writing, I experience a sense of tiredness and fatigue (calm-tiredness) that I reverse by exercise, a cold shower, and a redirection of my efforts by going to my office for a few hours to see patients. By late afternoon or early evening, I've learned to stop all creative efforts for the day since I'm beginning to display signs of tense-tiredness: snappiness, impatience, gloominess, and a restless fatigue.

At this point, construct a profile of your best and your worst times of the day. When are you at your best? If you're not certain, respond to the following situation.

Imagine yourself as a student in a course that you haven't been keeping up with. You're several lectures behind in terms of reviewing your notes and haven't completed several of the required readings. As you're leaving the class on a given day, the professor announces a written test for late the next morning. You obviously need several hours of concentrated study to get ready for the exam. Which of the following study approaches would be most appealing?

1. You relax for a few hours, eat a light meal, and then start studying. You burn the "midnight oil" for however long it takes to get "everything down," then go to bed and sleep until a few hours before the exam.

2. You also spend the day relaxing or exercising, and then eat a light meal—but instead of staying up late you go to bed earlier than usual with the alarm set for 5 A.M. When you awaken the next morning, you spend the next few hours studying and finish up about an hour or two before the exam.

If you chose to work late into the night, you're an owl. If you preferred going to bed early and getting up early to study, you're a lark. Now that you know which category you fit into, plan your creative efforts accordingly. Your most demanding tasks should be carried out during the hours of calm-energy and tense-energy when your brain operates at peak efficiency. The more routine tasks can be relegated to later in the day when you enter the early stages of calm-tiredness. Try not to do anything but rest and recoup when you're experiencing tense-tiredness. Nothing worthwhile is accomplished in tense-tiredness, and pushing yourself to accomplish anything while in that state leads to burnout.

Best of all, it's possible to convert from a negative state like tense-tiredness to a positive one like calm-energy or calm-tiredness. Simply stop all efforts and go to sleep. Even a brief fifteen-minute nap can shift you from tense-tiredness to either calm-tiredness or, after you've established the nap habit, calm-energy.

If you want to convert from calm-tiredness to calm-energy, go out for a walk. Thayer has found that if a person takes a brisk walk for as little as ten minutes, he or she immediately feels more energized and remains feeling that way for at least an hour. So how do you decide whether you should take a walk (the proper response to calm-tiredness) or take a nap (the antidote for tense-tiredness)? Again, calm-tiredness isn't characterized by negative elements like depression, anxiety, irritability, pessimistic thoughts, or angry resentment. If any of these are present, you're suffering from tense-tiredness and only sleep is going to cure it. If you're uncertain which state you're in, then try the walk. While mild exercise will dispel calm-tiredness, tense-tiredness will only get worse; ten minutes later, you'll feel additionally burdened instead of rested.

Although some authorities recommend certain foods as energy generators, I'm less enthusiastic at the promise of gaining unbounded energy as a result of eating a candy bar or a serving of vegetables. In fact, Thayer looked at the effects of candy bars on mood. He found that although subjective feelings of energy increased immediately after eating the candy, the energy level dropped even lower within an hour and, what's worse, was often associated with some of the feelings associated with tense-tiredness. Sugar, it turns out, is energy enhancing in the short term, but energy depleting very soon thereafter. But whatever your individual response to sugar, one thing is certain about the food-energy connection. If you want your brain to operate at its best in the afternoon, avoid heavy lunches, especially lunches high in carbohydrates. Diet and nutrition are important to proper brain functioning and deserve your thoughtful consideration. (I cover this subject in detail in an earlier book, *Older and Wiser*.)

Other ways of altering the energy cycle include drugs and social interaction. When taken in moderate amounts in coffee, tea, colas, or candies, caffeine leads to activation of the cerebral cortex and the release of the neurotransmitter epinephrine in the brain. Not only does caffeine increase alertness, but under its influence most people are also more attentive and can apply themselves better to those repetitive, boring tasks that sometimes can't be avoided. Actual enhancement of performance usually only occurs in persons who are already fatigued, suggesting that caffeine is most helpful in states of calm-tiredness. Caffeine may make tense-tiredness even worse because of its arousing and slightly "wiring" effects. This is especially evident among consumers of more than ten cups of coffee a day or their equivalent in tea or caffeine-containing sodas. The symptoms of "coffee nerves" are strikingly similar to tense-tiredness: a pervading sense of restlessness, difficulty in maintaining focus, and a free-floating anxiety.

Social interaction is the best energy generator of all for some people. If you're one of them, seek out individuals who are perpetually "up" and resonate with their bubbly, infectious enthusiasm. Social interaction can involve face-to-face contact or just time spent talking on the telephone. According to a number of studies, people with a high level of social interaction tend to be more energetic and in a better mood. Of course, social interaction isn't for you if you're suffering from tense-tiredness. You tend to shun other people and, in response to your irritability, people tend to shun you. Social isolation and withdrawal are regular accompaniments of the depression and anxiety that accompany tense-tiredness. So get rested, and don't take your bad feelings out on other people.

Energy regulation is so important because the amount of energy that we have available to us determines the level of challenge that we demand from our brain. Equally important is the level of energy that we *think we have*. Surprisingly, our own estimation of our energy levels largely determines our attitudes toward our future endeavors.

If you consider yourself endowed with a plentiful supply of energy, you're more likely to undertake challenges that involve the twin possibilities of high risk and high reward. If you feel chronically tired and energy depleted, you're likely to avoid challenges. In fact, your estimation of your energy level is highly correlated not only with your future accomplishments, but also your general all-around health.

In addition, self-reports of energy level serve as excellent predictors of physical and mental health. Thus, your feelings of energy can serve as both a symptom of your present health and a predictor of your future health. So if you're experiencing constant fatigue, feel generally worn out, or are lacking in energy, start with a general physical exam in order to rule out physical illnesses like thyroid disease or anemia. If all of the tests are normal, your lack of energy may be the result of depression. If so, your energy level is likely to increase dramatically after only a few weeks on one of the newer antidepressants that influence the brain levels of serotonin and other neurotransmitters.

17

Strengthen your powers of attention and concentration.

*A*ttention deficit disorder (ADD) has become epidemic. Increasing numbers of adults fulfill some of the criteria set forth in the *Diagnostic and Statistical Manual of Mental Disorders* (4th ed.), which is used by psychiatrists to identify various mental illnesses. According to this source, someone with ADD

a. Often has difficulty sustaining attention
b. Often does not seem to listen when spoken to
c. Often avoids, dislikes, or is reluctant to engage in tasks that require sustained mental effort
d. Often is easily distracted by extraneous stimuli
e. Often has difficulty organizing tasks and activities
f. Often fails to give close attention to details

Is the increase in the numbers of people with these traits due, as some experts believe, to greater recognition of ADD? Or is the incidence of the disorder actually increasing?

Based on my observations of patients, friends, and relatives—bolstered with some self-observations of my own mental functioning on occasion—I believe the explosive increase in ADD is real. It results at least partially from the influence on our brains of two products of our highly technological culture: television and the computer.

Television has fostered a shift in our brain's operation from linear, logical, language-based communication to an emphasis on images. In advertisements, on MTV, and even in news broadcasts, images of widely disparate events and people rapidly succeed each other on our screens. The aim is to create rapid motion and excitement, rather than the stimulation of logical or even coherent thought. One instant we may be looking at a picture of the site in Paris where Princess Diana's car crashed; an instant later we see an image of the pope blessing children in St. Peter's Square. No explanation is given why these particular images are paired. But explanations are not the point. The goal is the creation of intense emotional involvement via stimulation of the right hemisphere of the brain, which is specialized for the processing of emotions. The logical reasoning powers of the left hemisphere are neutralized by a powerful, image-based technology.

Both our public and private lives are now characterized in the post-MTV age by the dominance of images. "We have learned a visual language made up of images and movements instead of words and syllables," writes James Gleick in *Faster: The Acceleration of Just about Everything*. Gleick reminds us that for the vast majority of those who spend more time watching television, videos, and movies rather than reading, the masters of language are no longer famous authors but the technicians who create rapid-fire commercials or special effects and trailers for movies and television. And even for those of us who don't watch that much television, the availability of hundreds of channels induces in us what novelist Saul Bellow describes as "an unbearable state of distraction." In a speech given more than a decade ago, Bellow recognized the dangers to our powers of attention and concentration: "Pointless but intense excitement holds us, a stimulant, powerful but short-lived. Remote control switches permit us to jump back and forth, mix up beginnings, middles, and ends. Nothing happens in any sort of order. . . . Distraction catches us all in the end and makes mincemeat of us."

Another source for our ADD is the emphasis on a staccato style of verbal communication—that is, the sound bite. As television critics have been pointing out for decades, television does not lend itself to fine-grained analysis of serious issues. That's because television is an emotionally engaging pictorial medium that primarily engages the right hemisphere of the brain, whereas thought and logic involve entirely different parts of the brain, predominantly the left hemisphere.

As a result of this shift from words to pictures, from thoughtful reflection to emotional involvement, many of us experience difficulty when called upon to evaluate complex issues that require reasoned analysis rather than sound-bite-level responses. We concentrate less on issues and policies than on whether we can "identify with" a candidate, whether he "seems believable," and whether we conclude he "comes across" well on television. Thus, measures of sincerity now involve images rather than words. A leader is judged sincere on the basis of video performance as the image-based culture replaces words. Does the speaker appear sincere? Does she "project" an image of authority and confidence? The right hemisphere of the brain assesses such concerns, dealing less with substance than with perception.

In tacit recognition of this sea change in our orientation, television critics now routinely review major political speeches. "The shift is from substance to style, from left side of the brain to right, from concepts and ideology to perception," according to Eric McLuhan, author of *Electric Language: Understanding the Message*. This shift has also influenced our reading and writing habits.

When most of us think of writing, we think of newspapers, books, and magazines. Yet these forms constitute less than one-tenth of written material. Fully nine-tenths of the writing today takes place inside businesses. Nearly all of this is being done on desktop computers.

Although you have probably never thought of it this way, reading and writing on a computer actually has a lot in common with watching television. Both televisions and computers incorporate a mosaic of images, backlit screens, and near instantaneous speed. All three of these attributes, especially in combination, tend to engage the right hemisphere and thus generate emotional involvement. This, of course, results in conflict since words—at least the words employed in business communications—are intended to involve the rational, processing characteristics of the left hemisphere. Further, when words appear on a computer screen, the right hemisphere is called into play in ways that would not occur when you're writing or reading the same words on a page. Indeed, expressing one's opinion on the computer screen engages a different part of the brain than when writing or typing out the same sentiment on a piece of paper. This difference in brain functioning accounts, I am convinced, for such puzzling phenomena as those seemingly inexplicable transmissions within organizations of indiscreet and ill-advised e-mail messages. In such instances, it's as if the brain's critical faculty in the left prefrontal lobe has become disengaged.

This shift from left to right hemisphere processing has also resulted in a shortening of our attention span. "Using the emotionally involving right hemisphere instead of the linear and abstract left side has resulted in shorter attention spans," according to author McLuhan. Writing in *Electric Language*, McLuhan suggests that "we readers have lost the taste and the capacity for long sequences of words and chains of reasoning." This decrease in our attention span represents, McLuhan suggests, "a shift brought about by long immersing our minds in a milieu composed of TV and computer screens."

Computers also make it more difficult to distinguish raw data and information from knowledge. As literary critic Sven Birkerts observes, information must be placed into context before it can be assimilated and converted into knowledge: "We have filled the world with untethered information, more by many magnitudes than it held even fifty years ago, but for most of us it has become pointless bric-a-brac." Just as calculators can diminish our mathematical capacities, computers can rob us of the ability to synthesize the threads of data into the whole cloth of knowledge. "Basically we are increasingly entrusting to software the various gathering, sorting, and linking operations that we used to perform for ourselves and that were part of the process of thinking about a subject," writes Birkerts in his essay "Sense and Semblance."

The computer revolution has also changed our reading habits. As Birkerts puts it, "The shift from book to screen may, in its eventual impact on our sense of what knowledge is . . . be as transformative as the shift from Newtonian to Einsteinian physics." At risk is our capacity to immerse ourselves in a book and fully enter the world of the characters. Instead, we flit through the book like web surfers. I realized this in my own life several months ago when I returned to one of my favorite books, Henry James's *The Wings of the Dove*.

As a young adult, I had enjoyed James's genius for creating a world in which the "action" involves what critic Peter Brooks once described as "the melodrama of consciousness." In my youthful imagination, I had reveled in the delight of joining the characters as they spend leisurely hours engaged in intricately interwoven conversations held in quiet, dimly illuminated Venetian drawing rooms. During my initial reading of the book, I proceeded at an equally leisurely pace in order not to miss any of the subtleties of dialogue.

But on rereading the book two decades later, I found it difficult to exert the intense concentration that James demands from his readers. I found myself growing impatient at the slow pace, as well as distracted and mildly annoyed at what seemed like senselessly prolonged dialogues that served to establish points of fact and character principally through what an anonymous reviewer described as "minute, qualifying, cumulative detail." My attention began to flag after about fifteen minutes of reading, and I found myself thinking of putting the book down and going over to the computer to conduct a web search on Henry James with particular reference to *Wings*.

What was happening? Why did I react with such impatience to a book and writer I had once adored? Principally, because the world I lived in twenty years ago had more in common with the world described by James than the world I find myself living in today. Computers, especially word processors, shorten our attention spans and, I am convinced, can exert a harmful effect on our brain.

I'm not suggesting we do away with computers (I'm typing these sentences on a word processor). Rather, I'm suggesting that when it comes to using computers, you should balance benefits with limitations. First, you should do the necessary thinking, establish context, and only then turn to the computer to provide the data and information needed to flesh out that context. In addition, you shouldn't let technology weaken your powers of concentration and attention. Portable computers, e-mail, and cellular phones can wreak havoc on your ability to attend to the people you come into personal contact with.

For example, imagine the following increasingly common situation. A man and a woman are in a restaurant over lunch. They met for the first time one week before at a party, and each is interested in getting to know the other better. While they're talking, a basketball game is being shown on the television situated in the man's sight just above the woman's right shoulder. While she talks, he splits his attention between what she's saying and the progress of the game. A moment later her cell phone goes off, and over the next ten minutes her conversation with the man at her table is suspended as she exchanges information with the caller, who may be a continent away. At several points in the conversation, she pauses to make a short entry on her handheld mobile device. In the interval, what has happened to the communication between the man and the woman who, presumably, felt strongly enough about each other to have arranged their luncheon meeting? Well, assuming one or the other hasn't already walked out of the restaurant in a justified huff, each might point out to the other that he or she seems less interested in real face-to-face encounters than technology-mediated interactions. She might mention that prior to the phone call the man wasn't really giving her his full attention. One moment he was looking at her, the next moment he was looking over her shoulder at the basketball game. And he might respond that with the arrival of the call, she largely ignored him in favor of the person on the other end of the cell phone. And both may insightfully remark that more is involved here than just hurt feelings in response to poor manners. And they would be correct. Television images—especially when they're part of the background—have a tendency to capture our attention despite our best efforts to keep focused on the "real life" around us. And cellular phones split our attention between the immediate environment and a virtual, mediated environment. As a result, we are all immersed in what Birkerts refers to as "the great mediation." "We have put between ourselves and the natural world so many layers of signals, noises, devices and habits that the chance for . . . connection is very limited," he explains.

In summary, technology is creating a nation of ADD sufferers. One of the ways of combating this is to enhance your powers of attention. Here are some exercises I have found helpful for enhancing the powers of attention and concentration. I believe it's vitally important to learn and apply these exercises since a lack of concentration, a short attention span, and distraction all reduce brainpower.

As an initial exercise in improving your powers of attention, select, at random, a short increment of time, say fifteen seconds, and then set that time span on a watch equipped with a chronograph function. Look away from the watch and mentally try to anticipate the chronograph alarm to the nearest second. When you can do that, repeat the exercise at different intervals up to about three minutes. When you become skilled at this, set the function for a longer time, such as twenty minutes, and on three or four separate occasions during that twenty-minute interval estimate the number of minutes that have passed. Then check your watch for accuracy. For estimates of longer time intervals, set the watch and then continue whatever you were doing. But even while carrying out other activities, don't forget the timer. Try to anticipate to within fifteen seconds when the alarm will sound. Developing a keen sense for the duration and passage of time is an excellent exercise for developing focus and concentration. It is also an indirect measure of brain function.

For instance, depressed people greatly overestimate time intervals—a concrete demonstration of their frequent complaint that "time hangs heavy on my hands." A bipolar patient in the midst of a manic attack, in contrast, experiences events as accelerated. This sense of acceleration is the basis for the frequent complaint that there "just doesn't seem to be enough time." Alzheimer's patients lose the ability early in their illness to estimate time accurately; sometimes they overestimate, sometimes they underestimate, but in most instances they are far off the mark.

Even among people unaffected by any neuropsychiatric impairment, the ability to accurately estimate short time durations varies enormously. I'm convinced this variation is responsible for many interpersonal conflicts concerning "lateness" or one person's seeming unwillingness to be "on time." I've reached this conclusion as the result of the varied responses offered by different people to this question: "How long do you think it would take you to drive right now from this office in downtown Washington to the Pentagon?" (After determining, of course, that the person knows the location of the Pentagon.) Not only do the estimates vary greatly (at midday the trip would take at least twenty minutes even under the best circumstances), many of them are also nothing short of unreasonable. (One person estimated he could make the trip by car in five minutes—an estimate closer to the time it would take him to get his car from the parking garage.) You can increase your powers of attention and concentration by fine-tuning your time-estimation abilities with the chronograph exercises. Keep a record of your accuracy.

If you want to get really good at time estimation, pause at different times of the day and try to guess the time before looking at your watch. This exercise, incidentally, is not so much a test of concentration or attention but rather of your raw, unconscious time-estimation abilities, a talent you can improve by practice. As a variation, try to guess the time when you wake in the middle of the night. Most people become less proficient at this exercise in nocturnal time estimation as they age. Your efforts at maintaining that proficiency will help keep your brain functioning as it did decades ago.

The second attention and concentration exercise was developed for the Dutch air force to increase the attention and concentration spans of its pilots. The tests were used in the 1950s by neurosurgeon Vernon Mark to test U.S. Air Force personnel. Any random block of letters and numbers can serve for the test. The goal is to circle every example of a specified number and/or letter within a ten-second interval. A sample test is shown on page 143, where you should circle every 3 and every n in the block of random letters. You can make up many examples of your own. The trick is to come up with a richly varied mix of letters and numbers. The same example can be reused by selecting a different number and/or letter for each testing. Computer programs now exist that can provide endlessly varying patterns for recognition, along with a record of your improving performance. I suggest you take a look at one of the web sites listed in "Resources" for references to the available programs.

Another useful variant is the Symbol-Digit Test illustrated on page 144. The top row consists of the numbers 1 to 9 with a specific symbol above each letter. The goal is to write in the blocks the number that corresponds to the digit. At first, do the test as rapidly as you can with the key in front of you. If you forget the symbol corresponding to a particular digit, check the key. Each time you do this, of course, you lose time. But as your concentration increases you will remember the symbol/letter combinations and you'll no longer have to consult the key. When you reach that stage, cover up the key and do the exercise strictly from memory. When you do this, the Symbol-Digit Test strengthens memory in addition to attention and concentration.

The final exercise, the Stroop Test, assays an additional element of brainpower—frontal lobe function. Without normal frontal lobes you wouldn't be able to concentrate or remember. As mentioned under the discussion of the frontal lobes, working memory requires sustained attention to a stimulus during a period when that stimulus is out of sight. ("Out of sight, out of mind" is a perfect description of mental processing under conditions of frontal lobe impairment.)

As an example of working memory, a monkey is shown a cookie hidden within three shallow wells. A curtain is then dropped. After the passage of a varying period of time (depending on the experiment), the curtain is raised and the animal given one opportunity to reach toward the well containing the cookie. To do that, the monkey had to keep "on line" the observation of the well in which the experimenter placed the cookie. Normally functioning frontal lobes enable the monkey to avoid distractions and maintain concentration and focus. The Stroop Test is a pencil-and-paper measure of your ability to stay focused and ignore distractions.

To create your own version of the Stroop Test, you'll need several sheets of plain white paper along with three bottles of different colored inks (red, green, and blue). The test consists of three sheets. On the first sheet, write out the words *red, blue,* and *green* so that you have one hundred words in total, arranged in random order and with the letters printed in black ink. On the second sheet, place one hundred colored dots using a combination of red, blue, and green pens. On the third sheet, again write one hundred color words, but this time print each word in a different color than the color spelled out by the letters. In other words, the word *green* will be written out in red or blue ink, the word *red* will be in blue or green, and so on.

Take the first sheet and rapidly read the words without error. Then rapidly identify by name the colors of the dots on the second sheet. This should also not present a problem unless you suffer from color blindness. Finally, try the third sheet and name the color of the letters while ignoring the words spelled out by the letters. In other words, if the word *green* is written out in red letters, the correct

Figure K

CHARACTER SEARCH																						
1	7	5	c	g	1	f	g	p	4	8	d	n	r	s	t	f	1	6	5	3	2	8
t	6	4	2	4	d	4	d	c	t	d	g	h	e	d	d	g	a	c	e	s	d	v
d	e	v	f	g	5	6	7	2	4	3	4	6	6	u	c	g	u	7	8	9	o	f
v	b	b	m	s	z	x	2	o	d	e	y	f	s	g	l	f	f	n	f	r	e	g
e	t	j	k	s	w	e	r	t	y	i	b	x	s	5	6	7	g	6	s	w	2	4
6	8	f	y	k	l	s	x	3	s	1	s	d	c	d	f	e	f	f	g	h	j	k

Figure L

SYMBOL-DIGIT TEST

response is *red*. This will take two or three times longer because you'll find that your brain will tend to read the word instead of the color. The reason is that except for the artificial conditions of the Stroop Test, most of us have never previously encountered a situation in which colors and their word names are in conflict. As you will discover, a good deal of concentration is required to identify the color and ignore the word. Since reading activates speech and language centers, your brain focuses on words instead of the colors of the letters making up the word. Thus, the conflict between the word name and the ink color is normally resolved by your brain responding to the word and ignoring the ink color. You can easily see that this is true by measuring the time it takes for you to read the words on the first sheet, which are printed in neutral colors. This will generally correspond to your overall reading speed. Repeat the test on the third sheet while ignoring the word meanings and identifying instead the colors the words are printed in. That takes much longer because responding to colors rather than word names requires you to inhibit your natural tendency when reading to respond to words, rather than to the ink colors the words are printed in. It will require keen concentration and attention to counteract this automatic response.

When you successfully overcome this tendency to respond to words over colors, you activate your frontal brain areas, especially the anterior cingulate. The anterior cingulate functions as the hub for the brain's executive attention network. It involves the frontal lobes and its connections. Whenever you engage in novel or stimulating mental activities—activities such as the Stroop Test that require full mental alertness and concentration—you are stimulating that executive network. The end result is a heightening and enhancement of your concentration and conscious awareness.

Another test I recommend is a further refinement of the Stroop Test called the Color Go, No-Go Test. It consists of a series of cards with either of the words *red* or *green* written on them. On some cards the words and the printing are consonant (i.e., the word *green* is printed in green), while on others the words and printing differ (i.e., the word *green* is printed in red ink and vice versa). Each of the cards is also correlated with the carrying out of a specific action. I suggest a rapid knock-knock tap on the table as the expression of the Go signal and no movement at all for the No-Go signal. Tap each time and read aloud the word *green* if it's written in green ink. Do not tap on the table and remain silent in response either to the word, or the color, *red*. This should prove easy since you have a lifetime of experience as a pedestrian or a driver responding to green and inhibiting your actions on red. But when the word and the color it's printed in differ, you have to work hard in order not to respond on the basis of your previous experience. And the required inhibition is both verbal (reading out any word printed in green while remaining silent for words written in red) and motor (acting on green and inhibiting your action on red).

The above exercises challenge the brain in meaningful ways. Incidentally, the term "meaningful" is very important when embarking on brain exercises. While learning mirror writing and reading, for instance, might prove challenging, such an exercise isn't likely to prove beneficial since few occasions arise for exercising such skills. In addition, the brain isn't designed for mirror writing or reading. Such a mental exercise is as useless as taking up backward jogging. Whenever a person jogs in a backward direction, he or she works in opposition to the natural anatomical arrangement of muscles, joints, tendons, and nerves in the legs. Neither the brain nor the legs are programmed for rapid retropulsion. Such an exercise is not only unhelpful, but can also result in the tearing and damaging of muscles and tendons. Also unhelpful is the advice contained in supposedly authoritative books that claim you can improve your brain's performance by such silly exercises as brushing your teeth using your nondominant hand, or closing your eyes as you approach your front door with key in hand. In the latter instance, it's suggested on the basis of no evidence whatsoever that your brain will benefit when you have to use your sense of touch alone when inserting the key. While such quaint rituals might result in provoking your brain into a "What is this all about?" attitude, there is no evidence that such quirky variations in your daily routine have any effect on your brain's performance. Rather, it's more helpful to work with your brain's natural inclinations rather than create artificial "exercises" that make no sense. In *Mozart's Brain and the Fighter Pilot*, we want to enhance your brain's natural biological predispositions in order to enhance your brain's ability to concentrate.

18

Train your powers of logic.

*A*fter a coin lands heads up four times in a row, what is the likelihood of its coming up tails on the fifth toss? Although it seems reasonable to assume that after four instances of heads the odds favor the coin's turning up tails, the chance still remains fiftyfifty. And this remains true no matter how often the coin is flipped. The odds of coming up heads or tails remains 50 percent regardless of what happened before. In fact, when it comes to prediction you're more likely to make the correct call if you didn't know about the "run" of four consecutive heads. That's because knowing about the previous results increases the likelihood that you will trust your instinct that it's time for a change. In this instance, if you're wagering money on the outcome, your financial survival depends upon your ability to ignore instincts and stick with the odds.

Many people make similar reasoning errors when choosing which stocks to sell. Despite investment advice to the contrary, they tend to base their decision on whether they're holding the stock at a profit or a loss. Instead of selling off the losers and keeping with the profitable winners, they tend to sell the stocks held at a profit while holding on to losing stocks. Known among investment counselors as the "disposition effect," this irrational and illogical behavior can sink an otherwise well-planned investment portfolio. The stock, like the coin, doesn't know about its previous experience. Whether the stock is a good investment for the future cannot be determined by reference to how much was originally paid for it. Of course, the original cost will be a factor in determining how much may eventually be earned if the stock does well, but it is irrelevant to the question of whether the stock is a good investment for the future.

"Investors, it seems, will go to some lengths not to sell a stock at a loss," according to *New York Times* business investment strategist Mark Hulbert. "After all, as long as they avoid selling a loser, they can rationalize that it will recover some day, thus vindicating the original decision to buy. By contrast, once they sell a stock, investors cannot avoid the fact that they lost money." The antidote for the disposition effect? "The first is to understand that your psychological need to avoid losses may compromise your objectivity," suggests Hulbert.

As another example of our brain's tendency toward the illogical, take the belief commonly held by players, coaches, and fans that an athlete who has scored in his last two or three attempts is "hot" and therefore more likely to score again on the next attempt. Not true, according to the research of Cornell psychologist Thomas Gilovich. Scoring streaks do occur, but no more than would be predicted by chance alone. Gilovich arrived at this conclusion by analyzing player performances of the Philadelphia 76ers over an entire season. He found no relation between a player's performance on a given shot and the results on a previous or a subsequent shot. In other words, belief in the so-called hot hand is only a figment of the imagination.

As an additional example, imagine yourself a cabdriver with an income that varies from day to day depending on the weather, the number of fares, the level of tipping, and so on. Presumably, you would agree with the proposition that your goal is to make the most money while working the fewest hours. How would you go about doing that?

One approach might be to put in more hours on good-income days and quit early on days when you had few fares. If you followed this strategy consistently, you would increase your earnings by 15 percent. You would do at least 8 percent better if, instead, you followed a different strategy and forgot all about whether the day was good or bad and simply worked the same number of hours every day.

Yet New York taxi drivers follow neither of these strategies, according to a study led by economist Colin Camerer of the California Institute of Technology in Pasadena. He found that the cabdrivers do just the opposite of the most rational strategy: they consistently quit early on high-income days and work longer on slow days.

What could explain such "illogical" behavior? As with the investment strategy, most of us, it turns out, will work harder to avoid a loss than we will to achieve a gain. The cabdrivers have established in their own minds a daily income target; they will work longer and harder to avoid falling below that target than they will to put forth some extra effort to realize gains beyond the target. According to Camerer, "People open a mental account at the beginning of the day, close it at the end, and hate closing the account in the red." He believes we all have an "emotional reference point" that we have difficulty moving away from no matter how compelling the logic may be to do something else.

Accidents provide tragic examples of failure to apply elementary logical inferences. Smith, a commuter, is driving to his law office during the early morning hours in a dense fog. His visibility is confined to just a few car lengths in front of him. Suddenly, his car begins to sputter and choke. He pulls off to the side of the road and gets out. While he's standing in front of his car attempting to raise the hood, his vehicle is struck from behind by a truck and Smith is crushed to death under the weight of his car. As an intelligent and reasonable person, Smith was aware of the low visibility; that he was traveling on a main thoroughfare; and that under such circumstances standing in front of his car was extremely dangerous. Yet he ignored this disaster scenario.

While many of us might uncharitably label Smith's behavior as "stupid" or "careless," such epithets miss the essential point: the fatal disconnect between Smith's logic and his actions. Since Smith, like most of us, possessed no knowledge of the internal workings of his car, it was most unlikely that he would have been capable of recognizing a correctable problem by raising the hood and staring in at the engine. Indeed, that probability was less likely than the probability of being struck from behind by another driver who wouldn't be able to see him in the dense fog.

As these examples illustrate, the brain doesn't do a very good job when it comes to estimating probability. Here's another example with which everyone can identify.

Assume that you are planning on a Saturday to meet a friend for lunch. You decide to walk, a journey that will take about an hour, because you want to get some exercise to make up for the previous weekdays of physical inactivity in the office. Before leaving, you decide to check the weather forecast. You learn that rain is forecast for later in the day. Somewhere you've heard that on average, the forecasts are about 80 percent accurate. Does this mean that the chances you might later need your umbrella also are about 80 percent?

Actually, the likelihood you will need your umbrella is closer to 30 percent. That's because the *base rate* for rain must be factored into your decision. A certain probability of rain (high if you live in Seattle, certainly low if your home is in Morocco) can be estimated during any given hour. In this hypothetical, let's put the chance of rain at, say, about 0.1 percent. Thus, during your walk there is a one-in-ten chance of rain and a nine-in-ten chance that rain will not fall. Of one hundred trips, therefore, the base rate for rain makes rain likely on ten trips (100×0.1), whereas ninety trips will be rain-free (100×0.9). But remember that the forecasters are only 80 percent accurate. Therefore, of those ten episodes of rain, the forecasters will predict only eight. But that same 80 percent accuracy in predicting rainy episodes on rainy days also guarantees that the forecasters will make mistakes 20 percent of the time in predicting the rain-free days. Thus, they will mistakenly forecast rain on 20 percent (eighteen trips) of the ninety dry trips. Altogether, the total occasions when rain is predicted comes to twenty-six, despite the fact that rain will actually fall on eight of those occasions. So, despite the claimed high rate of predictive accuracy (80 percent), rain will actually fall only about 25 percent of the occasions when rain is forecast. So, despite the forecast, it's still more likely that you won't need your umbrella when you go out on your walk.

One final example. All of us, at various times, encounter people we have something in common with. It can be the same friends, the same astrological signs, or the same hobbies. In general, we tend to consider such coincidences unusual, even meaningful. Indeed, marriages and enduring friendships are sometimes based on feelings engendered by the chance discovery of such coincidences ("We really are soul mates"). Sharing a common birthday is particularly notable. During my life, I don't think I've met more than a handful of people who share my birthday, February 4. What conclusion should I draw from that? And what should I conclude if, over the next few months, after I start asking people about their birthdays, I actually discover dozens of people with birthdays on February 4?

First, it's necessary to make allowances for the fact that in most social encounters, the issue of birthdays simply doesn't arise unless one of the parties has an interest in discovering such coincidences. In this hypothetical example, I'm likely to encounter more people with my birthday if I actively explore this possibility with every new person I meet. But even if we get beyond this consideration, the probabilities aren't at all as straightforward as they might seem.

The probability of finding at least two people who share a birthday reaches 50 percent after the random selection of no more than twenty-three people—a reasonable number for a cocktail party or other informal gathering. The probability rises from 12 percent with ten people to 90 percent in a group of forty-one. So, the next time you're in a gathering of twenty-three or more people and you encounter two people with the same birthday, at least consider the possibility that the meeting of these two people wasn't preordained from all eternity but simply represents a fairly frequent coincidence.

But now consider a slightly different question: how many people have to be assembled in addition to myself to guarantee a 50 percent chance of another February 4 birthday? The answer is 253. Suppose we pick another date, say, April 10. How many people then do we need in order to find two people with that April 10 birthday? The required figure jumps to 613. What's going on? The large jumps from 23 to 253 to 613 occur because the last two dates are precisely specified (February 4 or April 10). In the February 4 example one of the people with that birthday (me) is already in attendance, while with the April 10 birthday we didn't specify ahead of time the presence of one participant with an April 10 birthday. In short, a seemingly improbable event (two people randomly discovered to share the same birthdays) is not really so improbable, but a specific *predictable-in-advance* event (two people with specified birthdays in common) is highly improbable.

Indeed, if you get any two people together it's likely that they can find many seemingly eerie coincidences in their lives. If they don't discover these coincidences themselves, an outside observer might do so on the basis of what he or she knows about the two people. In addition, an individual's interests and beliefs can serve as a goad toward uncovering seemingly eerie coincidences (the basis of many conspiracy theories, which place great reliance on seemingly "inexplicable" coincidences). But statisticians assure us that sifting through random data and finding coincidences not specified in advance doesn't prove much of anything. What's really impressive— and statistically unlikely—is predicting a specific coincidence ahead of time.

While the human brain filters vast amounts of information, it tends to consciously focus on things and events that appear unusual. This trait is a holdover from our ancient prehistoric past, when the unusual in the forest or the jungle often signified threats to life and limb. Better to flee based on the assumption that movement in the grass portends a predator, than to lose valuable time computing the odds in favor of other possibilities. While such an instinctual "hard-wired" strategy can be lifesaving in the savanna, it doesn't work so well when computing the odds under less harrowing circumstances.

Second, our intuition for probabilities is hampered because our brain's feature detectors respond only to the things that happen. Of necessity, we remain ignorant of things that could very easily have occurred with only a slight change in circumstances. For instance, if you run into an old classmate while you're on a vacation, you'll register that chance encounter and no doubt incorporate it into future remarks about the unlikelihood of such a meeting. But, perhaps unknown to you, all sorts of equally unlikely events didn't happen but just as easily *could have happened* with only minor changes in circumstances. Perhaps if you had stayed one more day or arrived a day earlier, you would have run into another classmate. Indeed, all kinds of improbable events may be happening that never come to your attention simply because either you're not around when they happen or they occur under conditions you're not prepared to recognize. In addition, too frequent a detection of weird and unusual coincidences sometimes indicates the insidious onset of paranoia.

My favorite example of benign paranoia involved a British intelligence officer during World War II who was among no more than a handful of officers with advance notice of the planned military raids on Dieppe, France. While paging through a London paper, the officer came upon an advertisement depicting a young woman in a beach coat trimming the thorny stems of a clutch of roses with a pair of hedge scissors. "Beach Coat from Dieppe" was the headline of the ad. The officer instantly interpreted this as part of a code warning of the incoming raids. "Coat" could be a shorthand for Combined Operations Attack—the very designation of the Dieppe raids. "Shears" could be referring to the planned British use of tanks against barbed wire. Finally, the number of buttons on the coat corresponded to the exact hour that had been specified for the first raid. When the officer hastily communicated his suspicion to his superiors, they correctly reasoned (and successfully convinced the officer) that the advertisement and the raid shared common but only coincidental features. All of us are susceptible to making similar logical errors.

Remember: since your brain is not a logic machine, be cautious when formulating informal probability estimates.

19

Develop a tolerance for uncertainty and ambiguity.

*U*ncertainty and ambiguity run counter to our natural desire for security, but they are indispensable for getting our brains to perform at their best. David Book, author of *Problems for Puzzlebusters*, spends days, sometimes weeks, thinking about the solution or construction of a successful puzzle. He's trained himself to handle frustration and uncertainty. Will his new puzzle be sufficiently challenging that his readers will persevere to the solution? When the solution is revealed, will the readers conclude that Book played fair with them and that the puzzle was worth the effort?

All of us are prone to what psychologists refer to as "premature closure": reaching a conclusion or accepting an explanation before carefully considering all of the facts and the logical conclusions flowing from these facts. Indeed, most of us are guilty of this tendency toward premature closure more frequently than we realize. Rather than tolerating ambiguity and working with it a little longer, we jump to logically incorrect conclusions. For example, consider this logical puzzle:

> Steve is very shy and withdrawn, invariably helpful if approached, but with little interest in people. A meek and tidy soul, he has a need for order and structure, and a passion for detail.
>
> Question: On the basis of that description, is Steve more likely to be a librarian or a farmer?

Most of us would unhesitatingly select librarian. Based on our observations of librarians and farmers over the years and in the absence of other information, we decide to go with a stereotype. But is it really true to say that we lack further information?

On a purely statistical basis, there are a greater number of farmers than there are librarians in the United States—perhaps at least a hundred times as many. Therefore, in the absence of any information at all about Steve, our safest bet would be to guess that Steve is a farmer. And that is exactly what most people do when presented with no identifying psychological characteristics. But when words like "shy" and "methodical" are thrown in people usually give more credence to stereotypes than probabilities. Most of the librarians we've encountered (usually on a superficial basis) *seemed* to conform to Steve's personality profile. Few of us have spent much time with farmers, and as a result we tend to believe they're all the same. But can a farmer not be methodical? Shy? Tidy? Why can't a farmer be taken up with detail, order, and structure? Of course he (or she!) can. But in the interest of resolving our uncertainty about Steve's profession, we ignore statistics (the base rates) and base our conclusion on stereotypes taken from real life and the media. (The description of Steve might well form the basis for a character in a movie of a male librarian—written most likely by a screenwriter with little personal contact with librarians.)

As another example of sustaining tolerance for uncertainty, consider this question posed to the editors of the British magazine *New*

Scientist: "Champagne will keep its fizz if a spoon is suspended in the neck of the bottle as long as the spoon does not touch the liquid. Why is this?" At first, the editors considered it unreasonable to assume that a spoon could keep champagne from going flat. But not wishing to appear narrow-minded, they decided to put the question to a quick test. To their surprise, they found that a half-full bottle of champagne left in the office refrigerator with a teaspoon slipped in its neck kept its fizz for twelve hours, and even remained somewhat bubbly after twenty-four hours. But before declaring their discovery of a new principle of physics, the editors suspended their tendency towards premature closure long enough to carry out another experiment.

This time they asked volunteers to blind-taste opened bottles of champagne that had been stored either with or without a suspended spoon. When the volunteers rated the "fizz factor" of different champagnes, the presence or absence of a spoon turned out to have no effect at all. Why? Because, contrary to most people's expectations, an opened bottle doesn't go completely flat until about ninety-six hours after opening. Try it for yourself (with a bottle of cheap champagne, of course). As a result, it's natural to assume the unexpected "longevity" to be the effect of a spoon suspended from the bottle's neck. The trick is to avoid coming to "surprising" or "extraordinary" premature conclusions without first suspending judgment long enough to test the facts and at least consider alternative explanations. As the editors put it: "It's not uncommon to attach significance to apparently linked events when they are rare and there is no control data. Every day you'll hear people say 'How amazing, I was just thinking of you and then the phone rang and it was you.' Although we would all like to be telepathically connected to our friends, what you never remember, of course, is the number of times the phone did not ring."

In order to break through our inborn tendency to leap towards illogical conclusions, and to counter the brain's comfort with nonlogical thought, we have to train it. One approach might involve a course in elementary statistics. As a less painful alternative, I suggest any of the fascinating books of Robert Smullyan. He is a professor at Indiana University, a magician, and, most important of all, an entertaining and instructive logician. In addition to the books by Smullyan, I recommend the previously mentioned *Problems for Puzzlebusters*, whose author, David Book, contributes puzzles to the *Washington Post*. Here are several of my favorites from *Puzzlebusters*.

The first is an old one that illustrates the important principle of keeping an open mind. Three salesmen arrive at a hotel in a small town. Since it's late and there's only one room left, they agree to share it. The cost is $30 (obviously this puzzle describes a situation dating from an earlier era). Each of the men plunks down $10 in cash and retires to the room. A few minutes later the desk clerk realizes he's made a mistake and that the correct rate is $25. He gives the bellboy five singles and sends him up to the room. Each of the men takes one of the dollars and then gives the other two dollars to the bellboy as a tip. Now the salesmen have each paid $9 and the bellboy has $2, for a total of $29. What happened to the missing dollar?

As Book points out, the key to the puzzle's solution involves understanding that two separate and unrelated processes are being merged into one. Try it yourself with thirty $1 bills. Put them into three piles representing the payments made by the three salesmen. Then introduce five more singles and distribute them one each to the salesmen and two to the bellboy. At some point the realization will dawn that there is no missing dollar. Adding what the salesmen paid to what the bellboy has is meaningless. One thing has nothing to do with the other. If you still don't get it, then change the scenario so that the men gave the bellboy no tip but simply split the five dollars into three unequal portions.

Try this one: "What occurs twice in a moment, once in every minute, yet never in a million years?" The key here is to think about the question in a different way. Moment, minute, and millions of years refer to units of time. But, in contrast to a minute, both a moment and millions of years are vague and difficult to measure precisely—a strong hint that the correct answer isn't going to come from analyzing the question in terms of units of elapsed time. What else do the three words have in common? At their most basic, all three terms are words. And words are composed of letters. Now the answer should pop out at you. The letter *m* occurs once in a minute, twice in a moment, and not at all in years.

As another example of how you must embrace ambiguity and resist leaping to early conclusions, try another puzzle: "Rearrange the letters of NEW DOOR to make one word." Before launching into the anagram mode and shifting the letters around in your head, consider exactly what the puzzle is asking you to do. Do it. The answer is ONE WORD.

I suggest that you develop an interest in similar word games. We are verbal creatures and our brains thrive on words. As we learn new words, we expand our mental horizons. Anagrams are my favorites, especially anagrams of other people's names. "Almost any name with a good distribution of alphabetic letters can be turned into either a flattering or an unflattering anagram of itself," writes D. A. Borgmann. "Thus Demetri Alfred Borgmann lends itself to the flattering anagram GRANDMIND, MORTAL FIBRE! as well as the negative anagram, DAMN MAD BORING TRIFLER! Try your own name and come up with positive and not-so-positive anagrams. But don't read too much significance into your results.

If you prefer crossword puzzles to anagrams, make them even more challenging by setting a time limit. Your brain will adjust after a few days and you'll find you've finished the puzzle in less time. That's because the brain operates at its best when given some basic instructions about the time available to carry out a particular task. And it can always work faster if you ask it to. So get in the habit of practicing what I call brain programming: setting a particular performance goal for the brain and then allowing the brain to achieve that goal without conscious interference or control. For instance, when I'm writing a book, a kind of word game, I try to write somewhere between five hundred and a thousand words a day. If I'm pressed for time, I type on the top of the page at the start of my writing session the number of minutes or hours that I am free to work. On most occasions, just seeing the amount of available time written out stimulates my brain to function more efficiently.

Think of word games and brainteasers (or logic games) as ways of getting your creative juices flowing and ensuring the channels to an open mind are kept open. They are, in fact, often included in job interviews with high-tech companies like Microsoft in order to spot "outside-the-box" thinkers. Here are several brainteasers, as they refer to them in Silicon Valley.

You are in a room with three light switches that turn on three lightbulbs in another room. You can turn any two of the switches on but you're allowed to go to the room only once to check which lights are on. How can you figure out which switch turns on which bulb?

The trick here involves breaking out of the mind-set that assumes you will go into the room to look at the three bulbs. The puzzle leads you to this assumption with words like "lightbulbs," "lights," and "turn on." But you have other senses, don't you? And since sounds, tastes, or smells aren't likely to be helpful, you're left with the most primitive sense of all: sensation. Do you get the answer now?

Turn two switches on for ten or more minutes. Then turn one of them off. Go into the other room. The lightbulb that is still lit is controlled by the switch you left on. Then touch the other two bulbs. The switch you turned off controls the warm one. The third switch controls the other lightbulb.

Finally, here is a particularly challenging puzzle from David Book: "How are the following objects related? A) cannons, B) footballs, C) gears, D) potatoes, E) shoes."

"Some problems are so formless that there's no way to get a grip on them," according to Book. He suggests that to solve such brainteasers, you should try thinking about the words of the puzzle in totally different, even bizarre ways. For instance, do the five words in that seemingly unrelated list share any features in spelling or pronunciation, as with the "NEW DOOR" puzzle presented above? What do you associate the objects with? What do they have in common? Where do you find them? Finally, do they have any parts in common? The answer is "Yes" to only the last of these questions.

In this puzzle, the five seemingly unrelated objects do have parts in common, specifically parts of the human body. More specifically, parts of the human face! Think harder; think "outside the box"!

Cannons have mouths. Footballs have noses. Gears have teeth. Potatoes have eyes. Shoes have tongues.

When you encounter a puzzle that intrigues you, approach it the way you would a koan. Keep thinking about it; keep it in the forefront of your attention; turn it over in your mind until it becomes as familiar as the feel of a favorite stone. Then put it out of your mind entirely until a few minutes before you go to bed. During the night your brain will work on the puzzle, and in the morning take it up again with concentration and vigor. The goal is to achieve a sudden insight, an "a-ha" experience wherein you suddenly discover a novel and pleasurable insight. Here is a final puzzle of David Book's to ponder.

> At opposite ends are my mouth and my head. I run for miles without leaving my bed. What am I?

You may see the answer to this puzzle immediately. If not, here is David Book's formula for solving it:

> Taken literally, these sentences are paradoxical. The key words responsible for their contradictoriness are "mouth," "head," "run," and "bed," all of which have several meanings. Try free-associating. Find another person or persons willing to discuss the riddle with you, or at least to listen while you talk. Sleep on it. Try anything that will keep the problem on your mind or close to it. You don't have to spend every minute on the project. Just a reminder now and then is all it takes to keep your unconscious riddle-solving machinery on the job. Eventually the answer surfaces.

For this final puzzle, the answer is "a river!" If you have enjoyed those, I have listed several books and websites devoted to puzzles in "Resources."

20

Develop your powers of metacognition: thinking about your thinking.

*A*ll of us possess strengths and weaknesses in regard to our brain's performance. By becoming aware of our personal assets and liabilities in our brain's functioning, we can gain what decision-making expert Gary Klein refers to as "the power to see the invisible." In his research, Klein has discovered that experts not only know more, but also observe more. For instance, a jeweler needs only a cursory glance to distinguish a diamond from an imitation. Such ability is based on knowledge, of course, but also depends on accurate and instantaneous perception. The jeweler's knowledge coexists with the perceptual acuity needed to distinguish accurately and quickly the genuine from the fake article.

As another example, consider a chess master who over his career has played thousands of games against the strongest players in the world. Success in any individual game depends on his ability to select winning moves. And the really accomplished player doesn't lose this ability under unusually challenging conditions. Even in games played at a rapid pace (blitz chess), the master's level of play remains consistent while the amateur's performance, in contrast, plummets dramatically in response to the narrowed time constraints. In this example, the expert chess player is able to respond accurately when deprived of the extra time usually available in a standard game for thinking through the various options at a more measured pace. In both examples—gemology and chess—the expert has learned to employ metacognition to manage personal limitations.

According to Klein, four components of metacognition are most important in thinking like an expert:

- Becoming acquainted with your memory and its limitations
- Getting the big picture
- Self-critiquing your own performance
- Effectively selecting the best strategy

As discussed in chapter 7, the first step toward improving your memory is to learn your present memory limitations. Do you carry a lot of telephone numbers around in your head? Or do you consult a notebook or a day-timer? In regard to long-term memory, is it likely you will recall several months from now the identity of the person who has just borrowed your favorite book? Will you even miss the book, the first step in initiating efforts to get it back?

Experts are aware of their limitations in these areas and modify their brain function to overcome them. At important moments when attempting to form a memory, they may increase their level of awareness or their ability to sustain concentration. Or they may set up corrective procedures like writing on a calendar or in a notebook or using other memory ticklers.

Experts are not only better at putting things into perspective, but also quicker at detecting when they're starting to lose the big picture. Rather than waiting until things have irreversibly deteriorated, the expert takes a step back from the situation and makes the necessary mental adaptations: "What is my purpose here?" "How did I get sidetracked and what's the simplest way of getting back on track?"

Many times your sense of the big picture can be regained simply by asking yourself these kinds of questions.

If you want to think and perform like an expert, don't shy away from self-criticism. If your performance isn't up to your usual standards, be open to various explanations. Mentally review how you felt at different moments leading up to a performance failure. Put aside your feelings of embarrassment and ego involvement. Your goal is to achieve the status of mental expert: master of your brain's performance. Experts in other areas do this all the time. By practice and custom over the years, they've mastered the art of constructive, tough-minded self-criticism.

Finally, use the first three components of metacognition—working with your memory limitations, focusing on the big picture, and critiquing your performance—in order to change your strategies. Draw up new plans and new approaches. If alternatives are slow in coming, start making a mind map either on paper or, even better, on the computer with the help of a program like Inspiration, the one mentioned in chapter 10. The key is to incorporate the insights gained from metacognition into action plans that enhance your brain's strengths and compensate for your brain's limitations.

Another equally important factor in metacognition involves your emotional responses. If you're like most people, you can readily bring to mind occasions when your emotions interfered with your performance. Perhaps somebody or something irritated you to the point that you said or did something you later regretted. Worst of all, your impatience or ill humor demonstrated to others that you weren't in control of your own feelings. At such times, your brain's limbic system overrides the rational, reasonable alternatives suggested by the prefrontal lobes. Here's a quick way to reestablish and maintain control over your emotions.

Start by observing your emotional responses at the present moment. Every thought is accompanied by what psychiatrists refer to as an "emotional valence"—a positive or negative limbic-based feeling. With most thoughts, the valence is weak and exerts little influence on our emotional equilibrium. On other occasions, the valence is strong enough to exert a decisive influence on mood and responses. Your goal is to train yourself to recognize the valence accompanying each of your thoughts.

As a form of exercise, train yourself to be aware of the early, subtle, emotional nuances that appear when you learn that a particular person has called you and left a callback message. Are you pleased? Or are you suddenly and "for no reason" feeling out of sorts? If you recognize and identify the emotional valence associated with hearing the person's name, you may find that your change in mood isn't all that inexplicable. You are responding to something about the person that you may not even be able to put into words.

On occasion, the emotional valence may be hard to detect. But it is always there if you stay attuned. As you become more skilled at detecting the first stirrings of emotion, you will develop what psychoanalysts refer to as the "observing ego." In essence, you'll develop the ability to observe your emotions with an objectivity that approaches the way you observe emotions in others. This will place you at a tremendous advantage when dealing with others in emotionally charged situations.

For instance, have you ever noticed that some people become angry but don't seem to recognize their anger and may even deny it if confronted? Such people aren't lying when they state they don't "feel" anger. They lack even the barest components of the observing ego. But by failing to recognize their anger, they miss the most essential component of their experience. In a phrase popularized in the 1980s, they're "out of touch" with their feelings. "The most abstract idea and the most philosophically sophisticated poem have feelings attached to them; without feelings there is no resonance, nothing of what we call meaning," according to poet C. K. Williams.

If you cultivate a finely tuned observing ego, you can enhance and enlarge your brain's powers to learn and profit from experience. The process is like what happens when you learn to appreciate the counterpoint in a Bach fugue. With experience, you perceive the musicians combining two or more musical parts so that you, as the listener, experience them as simultaneous yet independent lines of music. Psychological counterpoint works the same way: your thoughts and emotions remain separately recognizable yet woven together into a unified experience.

In the telephone callback example mentioned above, psychological counterpoint involves the simultaneous recognition and interweaving of your thoughts and feelings. You recognize your discomfort when you hear that particular person's name, but instead of ignoring the discomfort, you use it as an exploratory tool: "Why am I responding with anxiety? Is it because at our first meeting I felt a vague but definite sense of distrust? Why did I feel that way? And why has that feeling persisted?" Then, instead of merely wondering about your feelings, test them: "Perhaps it's time to really look at what has happened between the two of us since our last contact. I think I'll get out my notes of our earlier transactions and my feelings about them at the time and see if I find anything that justifies my present uncomfortable feelings."

Psychological counterpoint involves a synthesis of the operations of the brain's right and left hemispheres. As discussed earlier, your right hemisphere is skilled at detecting the emotional components of every situation. It specializes in the evaluation of tones of voice, facial expressions, body movements, and the "silences" between words. The left hemisphere operates in a "just-the-facts" mode that emphasizes logic and reason. Each hemisphere is equally important; as mentioned earlier on, we're not logic machines, but at the same time we'd be foolish to respond to every intuition and hunch that occurs to us. The observing ego balances these two tendencies and interweaves them into the equivalent of a Bach fugue. Our reason and emotions remain independently recognizable yet combined to form a unified experience. Both hemispheres are brought into balance: not too much cold logic, not too much hot emotion.

When you achieve an expert level of metacognition, you will become a "participant observer." Rather than reacting to your feelings, "acting them out," you'll be silently exploring the source of your feelings. You'll be asking yourself, "Why am I suddenly angry or depressed?"

For example, once while I was in a bookstore I frequently visit I felt overcome by an intense feeling of sadness. Nothing came to mind that could explain the depth or intensity of my gloom. When it reached a certain intensity, I felt the sudden urge to leave the store. But instead of taking action, I examined the situation. What could be causing this? Why was I feeling so low? I paused and looked around.

Nothing in the store explained my feelings. A handful of customers lingered near a bookcase just inside the front window. Outside the window, the accumulated snow from the previous day's storm glistened in the pale winter sunlight. And then suddenly the reason for my sadness became clear.

Last year at this time, also on a winter day with snow on the ground, I had come to this bookstore with one of my best friends. That friend is now dead. His end had been sudden, shocking, and brutal. At that moment, I recognized the surge of depression as my brain's way of reminding me of my friend and the good times we had spent together over the years. I closed my eyes and silently remembered him with all of the intensity I could muster. Within a minute, the depression passed. Later, after leaving the store, I called my friend's widow and told her what had occurred. Within a few moments we were joyfully remembering happy occasions when the three of us had been together.

As in this example, use your feelings as a stimulus for internal exploration. And don't hurry the process, despite the discomfort you may be experiencing. Remain confident that your brain will provide you with the answer that you're seeking. Often this may involve a sudden insight that occurs outside of conscious awareness. Remember that conscious processing is only a small part of the work done by the brain. The majority of the brain's operations do not require consciousness—indeed, as mentioned earlier, too much reliance on running everything through consciousness may work as an impediment rather than a stimulus to further insight. Learn to trust your brain.

21

Increase mental acuity through wide and varied reading.

In his book *The Year of the Death of Ricardo Reis*, Nobel Prize–winning novelist José Saramago wrote: "A man must read widely, a little of everything or whatever he can, but given the shortness of life and the verbosity of the world, not too much should be demanded of him. Let him begin with those titles no one should omit, commonly referred to as books for learning, as if not all books were for learning, and this list will vary according to the fount of knowledge one drinks from and the authority that monitors its flow."

But in order to gain the greatest benefit from wide and varied reading, you must correlate and synthesize what you've read. The best way to do this is start a reading journal. My journal consists of a leather-bound book equally divided into week-at-a-glance view pages in the front, and lined pages toward the back for narrative entries. Select one that is portable and aesthetically pleasing to you and provides sufficient space for your daily entries.

Each day, make an effort to read selections from literature, science, history, biography, or the arts. If you're like me, you will have to work these readings into mini-sessions. For instance, whenever a patient cancels an appointment at the last minute, I spend at least some of the time reading passages from one of the books I've chosen for the day.

When you finish reading, write the name of the book and the pages read on the appropriate date in the front of the journal. Then turn to the lined pages in the back of the book and list the key concepts and ideas you read along with your associated responses and impressions. If some short passage or quote impressed you, write it out for later use in the memory-enhancement exercises mentioned in chapter 7.

When something in that day's reading reminds you of an earlier reading, turn back to that entry and the journal pages written on that day. Then take a few minutes to write down the parallels you observe between the two readings, the differences, and, most of all, your own thoughts about them. Don't censor or criticize. Remember: You don't have to be an expert or hold an advanced degree in a subject in order to have original and provocative ideas about it.

Over weeks and months, your readings and journal entries will provide a record of your active and vital encounters with the authors of the books you read. The journal will transform you from a passive spectator into an active participant.

In order to get the full benefit, set up a special shelf on your bookcase for the books you've noted in your journal. That way you can quickly revisit an earlier reading and compare your present recollection with your earlier thoughts and writings at the time. This arrangement provides the most efficient filing system possible: books arranged according to your reading experiences. In addition, a bookshelf dedicated to the books mentioned in your reading journal enables you to meaningfully arrange new books as they are acquired and rearrange old ones upon rereading them. During moments of leisure, select a book from the shelf, think back to when you read it, and recall everything you can about it. Then open the journal, compare your recollection with what you wrote earlier, and write out any linking observations that now occur to you. This exercise is a practical application of novelist John Updike's point that "books externalize our brains."

Although I usually compose my reading journal by hand and my personal journal with the help of a word processor, you might prefer a word processor for both journals. The search function of a computer program enables instant discovery of links and continuities that in a written journal might take hours of exploration. Let me provide you with an example.

I was reading portions of Jacques Barzun's *From Dawn to Decadence: Five Hundred Years of Western Cultural Life*. In his discussion of events from the year 1500 to the present, Barzun writes that Leonardo da Vinci "does not deserve the title" of Renaissance man. Among Barzun's reasons for arriving at this harsh judgment: Leonardo never wrote poems or orations, had little to say about philosophy and theology, and took no interest in history.

Barzun's assessment of Leonardo is completely at odds with the opinions expressed in another book I read several years ago, *How to Think Like Leonardo da Vinci: Seven Steps to Genius Every Day*. In this book, author Michael Gelb not only declares Leonardo a Renaissance man, he also suggests that his readers can achieve the status of "a modern Renaissance man" by practicing seven "da Vincian Principles."

With the help of the search function in my reading journal, I instantly located my entries for the Gelb book and could compare them to what I was reading in Barzun's book, thus experiencing two contrasting views about Leonardo's status as a Renaissance man. The journal entries contained my own thoughts on the subject of Leonardo, as well as the relevant pages from the Gelb book I had read previously. These in turn influenced my thoughts about Barzun's point. I disagree with it, since the accolade "Renaissance man" doesn't imply that the candidate for such an honor has interests and abilities in every conceivable field of human endeavor. I expressed this view in today's entry, along with listing the relevant pages from Barzun. At a later point, if I encounter yet a third author who takes a position on Leonardo's Renaissance status, I can use the search function to retrieve both the Barzun and the Gelb entries and compare them to the third. None of this would be as easily accomplished, incidentally, using a handwritten reading journal, since I had forgotten about the Gelb book. But when I enlisted the aid of my computer's search function, the earlier Gelb reference to Leonardo leaped out at me.

But whether you choose the electronic or the written journal, over time you'll notice changes in your recall of the readings and your responses to those readings. In addition, your interpretations of the books may differ on second and third readings. This, of course, is to be expected. The brain is an ever-changing organ and today it varies greatly from its previous form decades earlier, so your impressions of a book read then are likely to differ from your impressions now. The written record of these changes serves as a means of personal integration.

As one of its greatest benefits, a reading journal provides a means of maintaining personal continuity in our fast-paced, rapidly changing culture. It's fascinating, and often humbling, to encounter in my journal prescient thoughts written years ago about a book that I can only vaguely remember reading. But it all comes back to me after a few minutes of reviewing my earlier entry, and rereading the passages selected during an earlier reading. A reading journal offers the opportunity for self-analysis, psychological integration, and objectivity. It can also provide challenge and enjoyment. Of course, the books will vary from one person to another according to interests and background. But as José Saramago suggests in the novel mentioned earlier in this chapter, "once we reach a certain stage in life we all read the same things more or less, although the starting point always makes a difference."

Whatever your reading selections, your goal is to provide your prefrontal lobes with material for the formation of working memory. Most of all, you want to achieve a deeper knowledge and understanding of human psychology. Novelists, dramatists, poets, and essayists possess an intuitive sense about the psychological aspects of brain function. Among the most insightful are Dostoyevsky, Stendhal, Charles Dickens, Shakespeare, Eugene O'Neill, William James (the scientist who thought like a novelist) and Henry James (his brother, the novelist who thought like a scientist), Thomas Mann, Søren Kierkegaard, Montaigne, Samuel Johnson, Jane Austen, Leo Tolstoy, Henrik Ibsen, Anton Chekhov, D. H. Lawrence, Marcel Proust, Joseph Conrad, and Virginia Woolf (who wrote both novels and essays). Among contemporaries, be certain to read such masters of psychological insight as William Trevor, José Saramago, John Banville, Muriel Spark, C. K. Williams, Michael Frayn, and Iris Murdoch.

Dip into these writers in any way that you're comfortable. Whenever I want to reread portions of Dostoyevsky's *The Idiot* or *Crime and Punishment*, I refresh my memory for the basic plots by referring to Cliff's Notes or Monarch Notes. That way I can enter the book at any point of my choosing. You can do the same thing on the *first* reading if you wish (although I think you miss a lot if you do). Referring to a plot summary after reading the whole book enables you to concentrate on the subtleties of character and the author's insights into human thinking and motivation. The important thing is to connect with writers who explain the human psychological condition.

Again, keep careful record in your reading journal of what you read each day (including the specific pages) along with your own impressions about the readings. After a couple of weeks, your journal will serve as a guide and a link to all of the books you've read so far. It will also provide the necessary continuity for linking your readings, as well as your responses to the different books. The goal here is not reading as many books as possible in a given time, but to incorporate your readings consciously so that you think of the authors as friends and advisers.

Let Dickens amuse you in *Pickwick Papers*, C. K. Williams stimulate you to rethink your marriage and relationships in *A Dream of Mind*, and Joseph Conrad entice you in *An Outcast of the Islands* into experiencing the Pacific Islands before travel became just another credential. But these suggestions may not be right for you; only you can decide. And your reading journal can aid in those decisions.

Your reading journal serves as a network linking widely disparate authors and books. This process mirrors what's taking place within your brain. It will provide a framework for working memory that you can return to again and again. Moreover, the books you're reading, when coupled with your accompanying reading journal, will, in the words of Harold Bloom, author of *How to Read and Why*, help you to "grow in self-knowledge, become more introspective, discover the authentic treasures of insight and of compassion and of spiritual discernment." And, in addition, you will be improving your brain!

22

Heighten your sensory capacities.

A s a first step, it's necessary to dispel several myths about the brain's operations during perception. Vision is a good example because it's the sense that provides us with the most information and, for most people, the sense they would least like to lose.

For years, experts on vision believed in a strict separation between seeing and understanding based on the following hypothetical model for vision.

The retina in the back of the eye conveys a visual impulse to the brain directly related to the frequency of the light reflected from an object. Thus, an object appears green if it reflects a specific wavelength of light corresponding to the color green. Once received in the visual center, the impulse is then shunted to a nearby visual association center that enables a person to identify the green object as a lizard. If the lizard moves, that proves no problem because, based on previous experience, a lizard can be expected to move. In short, the identification of the lizard, along with its color and movement, resulted from the synthesizing powers of the brain.

Brain scientists still agree with many parts of that hypothetical model. They agree, for instance, that different parts of the brain cooperate in synthesizing the perception of that lizard. But they no longer believe that the visual component of that perception is quite so simple. Instead, they've discovered that seeing is a far more complicated and interesting process that involves a merger of eye and brain, visual perception and understanding. Instead of two separate processes there is only one. This insight is a fairly recent one, incidentally.

Traditionally, neurologists and others studying visual perception assumed that following the transfer of visual information to the visual centers of the brain, other brain areas were called into play to interpret what was seen. In a famous nineteenth-century photograph illustrating the traditional belief about vision, an elderly woman who has suffered a stroke is shown staring at a sponge. She can't identify it by sight alone and looks puzzled. But in the next picture, she is shown smiling because she has just identified the sponge after reaching out and touching it. Neurologists at the time inferred that the woman suffered from visual agnosia, a term meaning a loss of the ability to identify what's seen (*gnosis* comes from the Greek for knowledge and the prefix *a-* implies the absence of knowledge).

In the eighty-plus years since those pictures were taken, neurologists have elaborated a different and far more fascinating theory of vision and its disturbances. Instead of culminating in a visual "center" that processes all aspects of vision, the visual experience is broken up into separate components such as color, motion, and certain aspects of form recognition. Thus, a person doesn't lose all aspects of vision at once (color, motion, form, etc.), but often only a single feature. As a result, injury to different brain areas produces more intriguing disturbances than simply a loss of the ability to recognize and name objects.

For instance, injury in an area known as V4 results in color blindness (achromatopsia). In this rare condition, the affected person neither sees nor understands color. Further, the person can often not even imagine what colors look like; colors simply do not exist for him or her.

Damage to a neighboring area (V5) results in loss of the ability to detect motion. One patient with loss of V5 on both sides of her brain found it impossible to pour tea because she was unable to see the tea rise in the cup.

In short, "seeing" is not a unitary process. Instead, according to Semir Zeki, who has pioneered the study of the visual brain, "there are multiple systems for processing different attributes of the visual scene." Moreover, he says, "these areas are autonomous and not dependent upon a central area. Further, activity in these autonomous areas can lead to both seeing and understanding."

I'm discussing vision in some detail here because I want to make the important point that perception, knowledge, and brain enhancement form a unified process. In addition, vision—along with all of our other senses—is an active process, not a passive one as scientists long believed it to be.

"Seeing is already a creative operation, one that demands an effort," wrote Impressionist artist Matisse. Painting, photography, and other examples of the visual arts also involve creative elaborations on the work carried out by the brain. As Semir Zeki writes in *Inner Vision: An Exploration of Art and the Brain,* "Art is an active process, a search for essentials; it is thus a creative process whose function constitutes an extension of the function of the visual brain." Zeki explains further: "We see in order to be able to acquire knowledge about the world."

As a practical application of these new insights into vision and our other senses, start sharpening your visual and other perceptual skills. In doing so, you will be enhancing your brain's functioning by creating new networks and enhancing your brain's representational powers. As a start, buy a bonsai tree—one of those miniature trees that share all of the features of a full-grown, mature tree except that its height is measured in inches.

Put the tree on the floor and stand over it for a few minutes, staring down at its branches. Imagine yourself looking at the tree from an airplane as it descends for its landing. Observe the tree closely, memorizing the form and patterning of its branches. Then close your eyes and try to re-create the branch patterning in your mind. Open your eyes and check for the accuracy of your inner image.

Now place the tree at eye level on a table. Study the tiny leaves and intricate branches until you can re-create them with your eyes closed. Your goal is to visually re-create the plant within your brain exactly as it appeared before you with your eyes open. With your eyes closed, visualize the bonsai in all of its intricacy and detail. Delve deeper and deeper with each try. Don't just visualize a vague number of leaves on a certain branch. Stretch your visualization powers until you can see the exact number.

Now stand up (with your eyes still closed), and recall the image of how the tree appeared a few moments earlier. In effect, you are challenging your brain to zoom out from a high-powered detailed image to a lower-power scanning image. Again, open your eyes and check your inner image against the appearance of the tree below. Finally, close your eyes, sit down, and visualize the bonsai as seen close up. When you've achieved the clearest image possible, open your eyes and check for accuracy.

The bonsai exercise is extremely relaxing, takes about five minutes, and hones not only your visualization powers but also your short-term memory, along with your ability to focus and ignore distractions. One important caveat: do not convert the image into words that you employ in a silent inner conversation with yourself. "Let's see; I think there were eighteen leaves on that branch but maybe there were only sixteen. I'll take a guess and say sixteen." Remember that you're engaged in a visualization exercise, not in an attempt to convert what you see into words.

Art provides another readily available and challenging means of sharpening your visual perceptions. In the next chapter, we will further develop this link between art and optimal brain functioning.

23

Learn about and experience art and music.

Learning about and appreciating works of art provide a marvelous means of enhancing your brain's performance. In fact, you can increase your brainpower directly whenever you go to an art gallery or attend an illustrated lecture on a specific artist or the art produced in any given age. I realized the interrelationship between art and the brain while studying the art of Salvador Dalí.

Dalí was the first twentieth-century artist to create double images: paintings that without any alteration of their components also represent a second, wholly distinct subject. In one of his paintings, *The Image Disappears*, you encounter a woman in a room with a map in the background. The painting looks very similar to a famous one by Vermeer titled *Young Woman Reading a Letter at an Open Window*. But if you stare at the painting and allow your imagination and perception to roam freely, you will discover that the same canvas also contains a hidden profile of the painter Velázquez. Thanks to this double image on a single canvas, Dalí united the two painters whom he considered the greatest artists in history.

In one of Dalí's drawings, *Study for Slave Market with Disappearing Bust of Voltaire*, a group of figures standing beneath two arcades suddenly switch into a second image: a bust of Voltaire resting on a table in the foreground.

Such double images are based on the fact that the brain can only hold one image within consciousness at any given moment. If you doubt this, test yourself with an optical illusion such as "the Salem girl/witch," the ambiguous woodcut described in chapter 8. At any one instant, it's only possible to see either the girl or the witch, but not both simultaneously.

Dalí employed double images in order to induce in his brain what he called "visual instability." Instead of taking common objects for granted, he suggested "misreading" them. A favorite example was the slow metamorphosis of the cloud shapes making up a moving skyline. Here is Dalí's description of the process as experienced while drifting slowly in a rowboat:

> All the images capable of being suggested by the complexity of their innumerable irregularities appear successively and by turn as you change your position. This was so objectifiable that the fishermen of the region had since time immemorial baptized each of these imposing conglomerations—the camel, the eagle, the anvil, the monk, the dead woman, the lion's head. But as we moved forward with the characteristic slowness of the row-boat . . . all these images became transfigured, and I had no need to remark upon this, for the fishermen themselves called it to my attention. "Look, Señor Salvador, now instead of a camel, one would say, it has become a rooster."

Dalí was not the first to point out that one should remain open to the magical metamorphosis implicit in everyday life. In his notebooks, Leonardo da Vinci suggested to the reader: "Do not despise my opinion when I remind you that it should not be hard for you to stop sometimes and look into the stains of walls, or ashes or a fire, or clouds, or mud or like places, in which, if you consider them well, you may find really marvelous ideas. . . . By indistinct things the mind is stimulated to new inventions."

In short, you can enhance your creativity by playfully altering your perceptions and trying to look beyond the obvious, most practical interpretations of what you see around you. By doing this, you will be improving your memory, imagination, thinking, and other cognitive processes through the establishment within your brain of new linkages and new networks. Art provides a powerful and enjoyable means of accomplishing this goal. So if you want to enhance your brainpower while stimulating your imagination and creativity, establish and maintain an active interest in art.

As Dalí and da Vinci suggest, allow yourself at least some time each day to interpret images, objects, or events in the world according to your own personal, and sometimes even seemingly irrational, associations. The brain is most creative when allowed to expand beyond conventional and confining ways of looking at the world. Even the senses can influence each other in unexpected ways. Leonardo suggested examining different surfaces and textures for inspiration, such as "walls and varicolored stone [which act] like the sounds of bells, in whose pealing you can find every name and word that you can imagine."

Music provides another means of sharpening your brain's creative powers. (I was first alerted to this by my daughter Alison, who is a professional harpist.) According to recent brain research, musical training stimulates and enhances brain circuitry. For instance, PET scan studies demonstrate that the cerebellum is larger in the brains of musicians than in those of nonmusicians. Encoded within that enlarged cerebellum are the fine-motor-control patterns required to play a musical instrument. And the cerebellum is directly linked with the cerebrum and its store of musical knowledge, learned over many years of professional development.

During a musical performance, the cerebrum and cerebellum engage each other in a dialogue conducted in intervals measured in thousandths of a second. Nor is this stored knowledge in the cerebrum localized—as previously believed—to only a few specialized areas. Expert musicians, including conductors, use widely dispersed though interconnected brain areas while intently concentrating on rhythm, melody, harmony, and other subtleties of a musical composition.

But you don't have to learn to play a musical instrument in order to enhance your brain's performance. Simply listening to music you enjoy activates parts of the frontal lobes and the limbic cortex on both sides of the brain. Music you find unpleasant or disturbing, on the other hand, will activate a different brain area (known as the parahippocampal gyrus) on the right side of the brain. As a result, those areas of your brain that are associated with pleasing music turn off. Thus, there is a sound neurological basis for avoiding music you find unpleasant while surrounding yourself with music that makes you feel good. Since people differ about the music they find pleasurable, your choice will have to be a personal one. Almost anything by Mozart is likely to bring pleasure, along with the opportunity for thoughtful reflection.

Listening to Mozart can also strengthen how you think and reason, according to Gordon L. Shaw, a physicist and the author of *Keeping Mozart in Mind*. "The more we understand about the impact of music on the brain, the more we'll see how important music is. We're aware of the emotional impact of music but it goes way beyond that. It has an effect on the reasoning and thinking part of the brain."

Shaw believes we are born with the capacity to process music. In his experiments with infants, he's seen them turn fussy if even a small segment of a Mozart composition is sequentially altered. Even at an early age, the brain is capable of subtle musical distinctions. And according to Shaw, this inherent ability to form and mentally manipulate patterns will continue to be enhanced whenever a person, of any age, listens to musical compositions like Mozart's Sonata for Two Pianos.

In support of this conclusion, Shaw points to experiments involving college students showing that short-term exposure to music increases the brain's efficiency in solving spatial problems. The above-mentioned Mozart sonata works best of all: "When you listen to it you hear something that's very cerebral, not just emotional."

Although some other researchers, such as Harvard University psychologist Christopher Chabris, haven't confirmed Shaw's findings, I'm convinced that listening to Mozart enhances the optimal functioning of the adult brain. My first personal experience combining Mozart with thinking and problem solving occurred at a conference on the brain held ten years ago in Baltimore.

After a morning of lectures on several complex and difficult topics related to brain functioning, the moderator dimmed the lights in the auditorium and we sat for about twenty minutes listening to Mozart. After about ten minutes, I began thinking of the brain in a series of images starting at the neuronal level and then progressing to the next highest level, involving specialized brain areas, and finally to the highest level of all, human behavior.

At the level of the cerebrum, the largest and most noticeable brain structure, information is encoded in the form of sights and sounds and textures—indeed, every sensory channel that informs us about the world outside our heads is called into play. The cerebrum, via its association fibers, links and integrates these perceptions into a unified experience. Simultaneously, the information collated by the cerebrum is transformed at another level into electrical, chemical, and finally molecular forms. Interrelations and correlations occur involving all of these levels.

While listening to Mozart, I reflected on the fact that each level of brain functioning exerts an influence on the other. For instance, a distortion in the DNA sequence in a person's genetic code can produce an abnormality in the brain that, several levels higher, influences behavior and results in a neuropsychiatric disease.

Two images then occurred to me: Russian dolls (*matryoshky*) and Chinese boxes nested within one another. Based on this insight, I wrote in my journal: "The brain encodes and decodes information on every level, from the smile and pensive last touch between parting lovers, to the equally passionate clasp of one chemical for another within the helically arranged DNA molecules that make up who we are."

Further elaboration of this theme led to my eighth book, *Recep-*

tors, based on understanding the brain in terms of frames and levels. I'm convinced this insight into the brain's functioning would not have occurred to me if I had not been listening to Mozart.

The bottom line: Try listening to Mozart for a few minutes each day. You will find, in Shaw's words, "music is really tapping into an inherent structure in the brain." Perhaps Mozart can help you develop the ability to engage in multilevel thinking and thus use your brain in more creative ways.

24

Organize a physical exercise program that aims at brain enhancement.

*I*n chapter 4, we discussed the findings of Robert Friedlander, the neurologist who showed that an increase in intellectual activities at any age offers the best protection against the later development of Alzheimer's disease. But Friedlander made another important discovery. Regular physical exercise also seems to exert protection against developing Alzheimer's disease. Taking other health measures aimed at lowering body weight, improving diet (increasing antioxidants and reducing fat intake), lowering blood pressure, and reducing the risk of blood clotting can enhance this protection.

While any physical exercise can improve your brain's performance, not every exercise is equally helpful. For instance, jogging and swimming exert a positive, indirect influence on general brain function by improving your cardiovascular fitness and your overall endurance. But neither of these exercises is *specifically* helpful to the brain. Since we're aiming for a brain-enhancing exercise program, we have to concentrate on three key concepts: balance, strength in the legs, and dexterity.

Many of us lift weights in an attempt to increase muscle power and tone in our arms and shoulders. And while lifting weights can tone the muscles of the upper body, it's even more important for brain health to build up the strength in your legs. Only when you increase the muscular strength in your legs can you exercise the brain's balance and coordination centers.

In order to improve balance and strength in the legs I suggest you take up tai chi, the ancient Chinese slow-motion exercise combining flexibility, bodily coordination, and lower body strength. But if you haven't the time or interest in learning any of the complicated, time-consuming, and often off-putting tai chi forms, you can get the same benefit from shorter versions. Whatever you choose, the key concept when practicing is to shift all of your weight onto one leg, assume a stable posture, and then maintain that posture. Here is an initial exercise that combines all of the brain-enhancing benefits of the longer tai chi forms and challenges the equilibrating and balancing powers of the cerebellum.

Start by standing with all of your weight on your left foot with the left knee bent in a one-quarter squat. Bend your right knee and extend that leg backward with the foot and ankle relaxed and with your toes pointing down and just touching the floor (see Figure M, on page 188). Hold your hands in the position shown in the figure. With all of your weight on your left leg slowly lift your right leg in front of you until your thigh is perfectly horizontal to your waist and your knee is bent to a ninety-degree angle. After holding that position for about ten seconds, slowly straighten your right knee. When the right leg is fully straightened, crouch down on the left leg as far as you can without losing balance. Hold that position for as long as you can.

After a few moments, slowly rise until the left knee locks. Place both feet on the ground. Relax. Stand on your right leg and repeat the exercise. Lift your left thigh to a horizontal position with the left knee bent at a right angle. After ten seconds in that position, slowly straighten the knee to form a straight line. Now crouch down as far as you can on the right leg and hold that position for at least ten seconds.

If you lose balance at any time, regain it by dropping the elevated leg to the floor and distributing your weight evenly until you're balanced once again. After a short rest of a few seconds, start the exercise again.

After several repetitions of this (increasing the distance you crouch down on the supporting leg), add one more detail to the exercise. Hold the position in which all of your weight is on your left leg, your right thigh is horizontal to your waist, and the knee is flexed at a right angle. Now bend your right arm at the elbow, bring it forward, and hold it in position a few inches above the knee. In this position, the bent right elbow and right knee should not quite touch (see Figure N, on page 188). Finally, while holding that position, gently swing the right knee forward and backward in an easy pendular fashion, all the while maintaining your balance on your left leg with a minimum of general body motion. If you do it correctly, your body will remain perfectly still with the exception of the pendular motion at the right knee.

After you have mastered this exercise, which challenges the cerebellum and the muscles in your legs, you are ready for the next exercise. Imagine a rope extending the length of the practice room. Stand on the "rope" with your left foot placed in front of the right and all of your weight evenly distributed. In order to balance yourself on this narrowed base, hold your arms out at your side at equal distances from your body (the bodily position of the beginning tightrope walker). Begin by shifting all of your weight onto your rearward right leg, then swing your left leg outward and backward and place it into position directly behind your right foot. While doing this, remain pointed directly forward with both feet on the "rope." As you shift the left leg backward, extend your left arm backward as well in order to aid in maintaining balance. After taking several steps backward, alternating the right and left legs, repeat the movements in Figures M and N. In one smooth, coordinated movement bend one arm at the elbow at the same time that you flex the leg on the same side, with

Figure M

Figure N

Position Check

1. Head and eyes—face forward.
2. Left foot—bears 100 percent of the weight. Left knee bent in a one-quarter squat.
3. Right foot—right knee in center of body, raised to level of solar plexus. Lower leg extends downward vertically. Foot and ankle are relaxed with toes pointing down.
4. Hips and shoulders—face forward.
5. Right hand—forearm and hand extend vertically above right knee in center of body. Elbow about two inches above knee. Palm faces right and fingers point upward. Back of wrist slightly curved (convex).
6. Left hand—slightly to left of left thigh, palm facing down and to rear. Elbow slightly bent.

the knee hanging downward at ninety degrees. If you do it correctly, the bent elbow and knee should form a straight line.

At this point, straighten the bent knee and elbow and move that leg backward to take its place on the "rope," with that foot now directly behind the other. In order to maintain balance while carrying out this maneuver, your right (or left) arm should fall to your side and move in tandem with your right (or left) leg as it moves to its position on the "rope." Shift all of your weight to your rearward leg and repeat the previous pattern while standing on that leg with the opposite elbow and knee bent and maintained only a few inches from each other. Keep repeating this alternating pattern until you reach the end of the imaginary rope.

Each of these exercises can be done at any time and even in cramped quarters. Simply shorten the imaginary rope and scale down the excursion of the individual movements. One caveat: As you will discover, these exercises put a lot of stress on the knees. If you have had a torn meniscus or suffered any other knee injuries, you might want to consult your orthopedist before trying these exercises. As an alternative, you can do the exercises in a swimming pool. This will challenge balance, strength, and coordination without placing as much stress on your knees.

In all of these exercises involving your whole body, the goal is not only to increase strength in the legs, but also to stimulate the cerebellum. You can also bring that tiny but important structure at the back of the brain into play whenever you dance, play tennis, or engage in any activity that requires smooth, coordinated responses.

25

Cultivate fine-motor-control skills involving your hands.

A large proportion of brain tissue is devoted to sensation from and motor power to the fingers. And enhanced brain functioning has been shown to result from improving, or at least maintaining, finger dexterity. Indeed, our ability to oppose the thumb to our other four fingers sets us apart from other species. That wasn't always so. Prior to about 60 million years ago, the hand was a clumsy instrument. But that changed when squirrel-sized early primates left the ground and began dwelling in trees. To accommodate that change, the thumb had to become more flexible, the better to grip branches. As an additional accommodation, nails replaced claws—thus making feeding easier. Finally, sensitive skin ridges developed on the surface of the palms.

At this point in your reading, pause and hold up one of your hands. Then rapidly touch the tips of each of the other four fingers to the thumb. With that simple gesture you have telescoped into one instant 50 million years of evolutionary development!

Ten million years ago, according to Frank R. Wilson, a neurologist and author of *The Hand*, our earliest tree-dwelling ancestors switched from the precarious practice of crawling across branches to the safer habit of swinging along below them. But swinging required a loosening of the attachment between the wrist and the ulna, the major forearm bone. This modification allowed for extra arm twist and wrist tilt.

Five million years ago, something very similar to our hand appeared on the scene. Our earliest ancestor, the famous "Lucy," walked on her two hind legs and could join her thumb, index finger, and middle finger to form a three-pronged grip that allowed her to pick up and handle unevenly shaped objects, such as stones. She could also use her new wrist and hand arrangement for pounding nuts with those stones. With her hands no longer required for motion thanks to her upright posture, Lucy could use her arms and hands to throw stones at her enemies. As a final alteration in the human hand, early hominoids developed the ability to oppose the pinkie and ring finger to the thumb.

Accompanying these changes in the hand were equally drastic changes in the human brain. Swinging from branches, balancing on two feet, examining small objects by opposing the other fingers to the thumb—all of these developments led to enhanced eye-hand coordination and increasingly complex circuitry within the cerebellum. The cerebellum maintains balance and links with those parts of the cerebrum dedicated to thinking. At all times, the tree-swinger and the later hunter-gatherer both required a refined kinesthetic sense to provide moment-by-moment feedback on the positions of arms, hands, and legs. The result of all these changes? A bigger brain marked by enhanced specialization.

Figure O, on page 192, is an artist's rendering of the brain's functional organization. Notice the large areas in both the sensory and motor cortices that are exclusively dedicated to the hand. Other large areas are devoted to the lips and tongue—the organs of speech. What could be more natural, since we differ from other creatures principally on the basis of our hand dexterity and speech?

The hand is the primary instrument that carries out the motor commands of the brain. In fact, the hand is best thought of as an extension of the brain. And the brain is first and foremost specialized for action. The frontal lobes are constantly formulating action plans that are transferred to the premotor and motor areas. When the plan of action is finally formulated it's the human hand, either directly or through some mechanical intermediary, that carries out the brain's desires.

At every waking moment, feedback exists between the hands and

Figure O

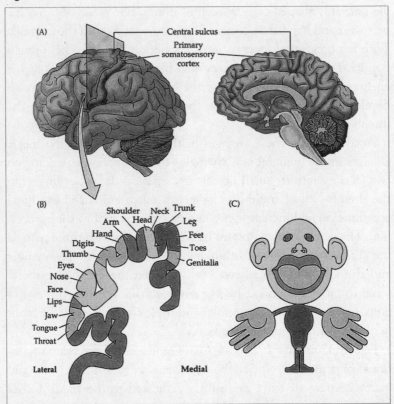

Figure O The bizarre and distorted creature that results when parts of the human body are drawn in proportion to the amount of brain tissue that serves each part.

the brain. Because of this feedback, brain performance and hand dexterity are intimately coupled. As mentioned earlier in reference to musicians, improvements in performance are accompanied by beneficial reorganizations within the brain.

The bottom line? Development of your manual skills will result in the establishment of new circuits in widely dispersed brain areas. What's more, these areas will become involved in extensive two-way communications with even more brain areas. Remember that skilled musicians activate widely separated though interconnected areas by reading music and even just mentally rehearsing a musical score. Moreover, these areas in both hemispheres are linked with brain areas involved in sight, touch, and form. The skills of the sculptor and the fashion designer are practical applications of the brain's organization. Both workers combine manual dexterity with an appreciation of form, texture, and design.

But as a result of today's increased mechanization and mass production, not many things are made by hand anymore. Indeed, we're living in an age when the human hand is becoming redundant. This holds true even in professions traditionally associated with highly evolved motor skills. For instance, medical personnel who possess no more than average hand dexterity can now perform surgery via computers. And writers may soon be replacing their typewriters and word processors with sophisticated speech recognition systems. As a result of such changes, a large part of the brain will undergo a form of disuse atrophy.

As another example of the intimate interplay involving manual dexterity, skill, and knowledge, contrast a neurosurgeon to a neurologist like myself who does not operate and possesses underdeveloped surgical skills. The neurosurgeon can literally close his eyes and see, in his imagination, intricate details of brain anatomy that are impossible to visualize for anyone who has not surgically explored the brain via hand-controlled instruments. The previous operations carried out by the neurosurgeon created dynamic functional connections involving the motor, sensory, and association cortex within the neurosurgeon's brain. But the most important link is with the frontal lobes—those parts of the brain that set up the premotor programs that will make a successful operation possible.

Which manual skill would I suggest? (No, I'm not suggesting you take up brain surgery.) The choice is a personal one. Anything that involves precision, attention to detail, sustained fine finger control, and—most important of all—the possibility for failure if everything isn't done just right. Included here: the construction of model airplanes, trains, and boats (in a bottle for a particular challenge), or learning to repair your own computer (after backing up all the files, of course) or bicycle. But choose cautiously and thoughtfully.

If you're thirty years or older and work in a sedentary profession that makes few demands on your finger dexterity, avoid taking up any activity involving power tools or other potentially dangerous equipment or situations. Your goal is brain-hand enhancement—a goal not at all furthered by the loss of one of your fingers.

Performing magic tricks provides multiple ways of improving your manual skills. Visit a local magic shop and ask one of the employees to demonstrate a few tricks involving cards or coins. In order to get started, ask that the tricks be simple enough for a beginner yet provide a gradual increase in manual dexterity skill. As your skill level increases, learn some examples of close-up magic. In this demanding genre, you perform the trick while sitting at a table with your audience sitting directly across from you. From here, go on to magic tricks involving card sleights, handkerchiefs, eggs, sponge balls, and silks. If you're like me, you may find these tricks so helpful in learning finger dexterity that you'll join the International Brotherhood of Magicians. Although many of the members of that organization are professionals, I can personally attest that they welcome amateurs to their meetings. Once you're a member, you can receive instruction on magic arts like card manipulation and, my personal favorite, mentalism. But whatever you choose, practicing magic can provide you with a fun way of improving both your finger dexterity and your brain's performance.

Some computer games provide another way of enhancing fine-motor-control skills and eye-hand coordination. Despite many of the criticisms of computer games (the fostering of short attention spans, the "wasting" of time that could profitably be applied to reading or learning other skills, etc.), there is definitely a place for some of them, particularly games simulating real experiences such as flying an airplane or driving a racing car. For one thing, such games demand a shift from left to right hemisphere functioning. Recognition of patterns, speed of response, and rapid coordinated movements are rewarded.

A personal favorite among finger-dexterity enhancers is the game Jackstraw, a variation of Pick Up sticks using color-coded sticks. The object of the game is to pick up sticks with the highest level of points without disturbing the others. Just one false move and you've lost the game!

But whatever manual activity you choose, keep in mind that training the hands in fine motor skills is really aimed at enhancing brain performance. A study of surgical skills among Canadian surgeons revealed that "visuospatial perceptual skills [the ability to mentally represent the physical environment and the movements to be performed] are the major determinants of surgical technical performance." The authors suggested that "learners should make use of learning strategies that improve mental representation of a skill and the corresponding anatomy," and suggested strategies like imagery and mental practice.

I mentioned a moment ago the construction of model airplanes or trains. In earlier times the exercise of similar manual skills provided a dependable means for understanding a model's design and inner workings. In *On the Art of Building*, Renaissance architect Leon Battista Alberti captured the process whereby the hand informs the brain.

I will never tire of recommending the custom, practiced by the best architects, of preparing not only drawings and sketches, but also models of wood or any other material. These enable us to examine the work as a whole. I have often conceived of projects in the mind that seemed quite commendable at the time; but when I translated them into drawings, I found several errors in the very parts that delighted me most...when I pass from drawings to the model, I sometimes notice further mistakes.

In short, manual and mental skills are not opposed to each other, but form a continuum. By enhancing your finger-and-hand motor dexterity, you boost your brainpower. So practice your chosen manual skill enough to establish and maintain the brain circuits devoted to that skill. By practicing, even just a little each week, you will be able to maintain complex networks of nerve cell interactions. And in response to your practice, the neurons in your brain will grow microscopic filaments that will connect to one another in the process neuroscientists refer to as arborization. As you progress further in your skill level, or when you master new manual skills, the brain secretes growth hormones and other chemicals that foster additional arborization. But you have to maintain your skill levels. If you fall behind in your practice, these filaments wither away (although they will not die off completely).

How much practice is enough? Although there are no hard-and-fast rules, remember that even a short practice period is better than no practice at all. The frequency and duration of your practice should also be dictated by your purpose. The majority of adults learn to play a musical instrument or construct models solely for relaxation and enjoyment. In most instances, these activities remain avocations rather than a means of earning a livelihood.

As one's skill level increases, so does the pleasure gained from exercising that skill. Cartoons and situation comedies frequently lampoon the husband (or wife) who devotes every spare minute to golf or tennis. "Why are you out there doing the same thing day after day? Doesn't it get boring?" asks the spouse. But of course the player isn't doing the "same thing" each time. Each round of golf or game of tennis is different, but these differences are lost on someone who doesn't play these games.

Remind yourself of your goals and realize your limitations. Unless you're changing careers, you're not aiming at professional levels of performance. So don't hold yourself to overly demanding standards. You're not out to become a "champion" or outperform other "competitors." In fact, you're not engaged in a competition, least of all a competition against yourself (comparing how well you did today with your past performances). Your goal is to establish and enhance your brain's performance by maintaining your manual skill levels in an area of your own choosing.

26

Regularly practice some form of mental relaxation.

hile meditation is another word for resting the mind, I prefer *relaxation* since meditation carries with it so much extra baggage. Your purpose is not the achievement of a form of mystical communion, but a respite for the brain, an antidote for stress and overstimulation. Recent brain research has turned up some interesting and even alarming facts about the effects of stress on the brain. As discussed in chapter 15, *stress causes brain damage*.

Hormones secreted in the body in response to stress produce a loss of volume in the hippocampus, an important structure in the formation of memory. The opposite also holds true: stress reduction enhances brain functioning. The best ways of reducing stress?

The first involves something we do several times a minute throughout our lives—breathing. Nothing could be easier, right? Actually, few of us know how to breathe correctly and healthily. Before reading any further, try this test. While sitting where you are, take in a deep breath and then let it out. Now repeat the process while observing whether your chest or your abdomen expanded on the in-breath. If you're like most people, your chest expanded while your abdomen contracted. But "chest breathing" is all wrong; it's bad for your general health, and it's likely to lead to an increase rather than a decrease in stress.

If you want a model for correct breathing, watch a baby breathe. The chest moves very little, but the belly goes up and down in a slow, rhythmic motion. Unfortunately, most of us switch toward chest breathing as we grow older ("suck in that belly, puff out that chest, and stand tall," as many of us have been told over the years). But this shallow, chest breathing pattern forces the lungs to work harder in order to provide sufficient oxygen flow. It also speeds up the heart so that it can pump sufficient oxygen-rich blood for distribution throughout the body. But since only the upper and middle portions of the lungs are being used, optimal oxygen transport doesn't take place. The result is a stress cycle: shallow breathing leads to additional stress, which accelerates the breathing pattern and leads to even more stress. The answer? Learn how to transform yourself from a shallow "chest breather" to a healthy "abdominal breather."

In their book *Healing Moves: How to Cure, Relieve, and Prevent Common Ailments with Exercise*, Carol and Mitchell Krucoff suggest the following three exercises:

1. Lie on your back and place a book on your belly. Relax your stomach muscles and inhale deeply into your abdomen so that the book rises. When you exhale, the book should fall. You'll still be bringing air into your upper chest, but now you're also bringing air down into the lower portion of your lungs and expanding your entire chest cavity.

2. Sit up and place your right hand on your abdomen and your left hand on your chest. Breathe deeply so that your right "abdominal" hand rises and falls with your breath, while your left "chest" hand stays relatively still. Breathe in through your nose, and out through

your nose or mouth; spend a few minutes enjoying the sensation of abdominal breathing.

3. Place a timer or clock with a second hand in clear view. Breathe in slowly, filling your abdomen, as the timer counts off five seconds. Then breathe out slowly to the same count of five.

These breathing exercises can be done at any time, especially when you're feeling stress. To gain an additional benefit, the Krucoffs suggest combining the breathing exercise with the mental recitation of a phrase of your choosing. This can be a short religious phrase or one that conveys a special meaning for you, such as "In peace, out anger."

The second stress-reducing exercise involves changing mental perspective, what psychologists call reframing. In *Magister Ludi: The Glass Bead Game*, Hermann Hesse described the process: ". . . review[ing] each official day, noting what had been well done or ill done, feeling his own pulse, as meditation teachers call this practice, that is, recognizing and measuring one's own momentary situation, state of health, the distribution of one's energies, one's hopes and cares—in a word, seeing oneself and one's daily work objectively and carrying nothing unresolved on into the night and the next day."

Here are two exercises for enhancing and integrating your brain so that it will remain active, dynamic, and less imperiled by stress.

The first I discovered years ago while sitting in a classroom listening to a boring lecture. It seemed like the teacher was going to talk forever. In desperation for something to do, I looked up at the front of the room and quickly took in the general configuration, including the exact arrangement of the students sitting in the first few rows. I then closed my eyes and tried to image everything. I repeated the process to include even more rows of students until I could see in my mind's eye a near perfect representation of the whole room. You can do the same wherever you are.

Focus as attentively as possible on whatever is before you at the moment. Over the next minute, memorize as many details as possible. Then close your eyes and mentally image the entire scene.

When you can't add anything else to your mental snapshot, open your eyes and check for all of the things you've missed. Repeat the process until you create in your mind a complete mental picture. Close your eyes again and see how long you can hold that image in awareness. Within a minute or two you will be conscious of feelings of boredom. Try to fight those feelings. Your purpose now is twofold: the combining of imaging accuracy with the maintenance of mental focus. After a few more moments, depending on how long you've practiced this exercise, you will gradually lose clarity and the image will fade. Take this as the current outer limit that you will enlarge by additional practice.

Contrary to what you might expect, this imaging exercise provides relief from mental fatigue rather than worsens it. That's because during the exercise, you are shifting from left-hemisphere language processing to right-hemisphere image generation. (Don't list the items, *see them* in your mind's eye.) Unlike the dolphin or the whale, we cannot shut down one hemisphere or the other, but we can shift the functional balance. The result is an infusion of mental energy.

The second exercise you can do at home. No matter how crowded your living arrangements, try to find a place where at certain times you can be alone. Sit comfortably in a chair and let your mind wander. Don't try to think any particular thoughts or dwell on a specific subject. The goal is to blur the boundaries between outside and inside. Sometimes sitting by a window and listening to the rain or the wind in the trees, or even the drone of air conditioners if you live in a crowded city, can help you to achieve this purpose. Nor do you have to be in familiar surroundings. Writer Ray Bradbury tunes his brain while riding on trains.

"I get some of my best ideas on trains. When I stare out the window it's an immense, unrolling Rorschach test. It's a long strip of paper on two rolls, like the theatres we used to build when we were kids." On the train, Bradbury lets his memory roam freely, sometimes to his earliest experiences. "It brings back memories. And then, you begin to cross-pollinate ideas from your past and it romances you into a certain kind of nostalgia and then the ideas begin to pop to the surface. Like myself going down the track."

In this second exercise, follow Bradbury's example and don't try to direct your thoughts in any way—at least initially. This is different from the first exercise, in which you are sticking with a single image or reflection. Here you're trying to do just the opposite: Allow your mind to wander and permit "the flow of inner images to come without direction, as they do, like in dreams, in the initial stage of relaxation" as Hesse describes the process.

If you experience initial difficulties with either of these two exercises, don't try to force the process. The idea is to let go, to relax—not to tighten mental tethers. But be forewarned: immersing oneself in one's own mental landscape is not easy in our present culture. When traveling, I used to do these exercises while sitting in the airport between planes. But now television monitors, set up at strategic positions in many of the larger airports, provide a constant distracting drone of infomercials, newsbreaks, and advertisements that interfere with the free flow of associations needed to make this exercise work. The self-reflecting mind described by Hesse is on the endangered species list.

If you get restless or uncomfortable doing any of these exercises at home or some other private place, get up and stand quietly for a few minutes. Center yourself by doing slow-motion exercises. You don't have to engage in formal tai chi forms—just any movements that involve weight shifting and balance. The movements described in chapter 24 work for me just fine. After a few minutes of carrying out the movements, pick up a pair of weights and repeat the movements. While doing so, imagine yourself moving in water. Under conditions of overstimulation, you can dispel mental distractions by focusing entirely on the movements. After a few minutes doing the exercises, you will be ready to sit down again and pick up where you left off without the previous sense of distraction.

If exercises don't appeal to you, simple standing can provide a marvelous degree of brain activation. In an experiment at the Positron Medical Center in Hirakuchi, Japan, volunteers adopted several postures while hooked up to a PET scan. They started in a supine relaxed position. They then stood with their feet together and eyes open or closed. Finally, they stood either on one foot or in a straight line with the two feet together in a "tandem" relationship (i.e., the toe of the backward foot directly behind the heel of the forward foot).

Compared with the supine position, standing with the feet together activated the anterior cerebellum and the right visual cortex. Standing on one foot increased cerebral blood flow in the anterior cerebellum and the cortex on the weight-bearing side. Standing in tandem activated the visual association cortex, the cerebellum, and the midbrain. Finally, standing with eyes closed activated the prefrontal cortex.

In summary, simple standing exercises exert a widespread effect on brain activation, involving everything from the balance centers in the cerebellum, to the vision and visual association areas, to the most advanced brain areas in the prefrontal cortex.

The Japanese findings illustrate the important health benefits that can accrue from simple standing exercises. These findings are already being put into practice in many hospitals where, if at all possible, patients are persuaded to leave their beds on a daily basis. Simply by standing at their bedsides and balancing themselves, the patients can reap the benefits of a brain workout. For those of us who are neither sick nor in a hospital, standing and weight-shifting exercises can act as a tonic, an activator that brings widely dispersed areas of the brain into play.

Another important component of stress reduction and mental relaxation is learning to turn the brain off and get to sleep. Indeed, if you want your brain to perform optimally, you must get sufficient restful sleep. But in our fast-paced society this isn't always so easy. On occasion, all of us are required to sacrifice sleep in the interests of career success. While we may pay lip service to the old adage "early to bed, early to rise," many of us work late into the night and then, after a restless few hours of tossing and turning, stumble out of bed into the predawn darkness, headed toward another day of intense work. The ensuing sleep debts that we accumulate make us more irritable and harder to live with, and may increase the chances of a heart attack or the development of a stress-related illness like high blood pressure or tension headaches. In addition, poor sleep translates into decreased mental efficiency. The National Sleep Foundation estimates the cost of employee fatigue at $18 billion a year.

And yet, realistically, sometimes you may have no alternative other than to "burn the midnight oil" and report to work the next day sleep deprived. Perhaps a marketing report simply must be finished for the 10:00 A.M. staff meeting. Or an important, hastily arranged meeting can't be put off. And what's even more stressful, you have to prepare for probing, even hostile, questions. The solution? Do your best in the meeting and then retire to your office for a nap.

Many of us associate naps with the opposite ends of the life span: early childhood and retirement. Actually, if weekends are included, 33 percent of adults take naps over any two-week period of observation. According to one workplace survey, people may benefit from naps but don't take them. In a second workplace survey, about 30 percent admit that sleepiness is affecting their job performance (since the two surveys weren't correlated, nobody knows how much of a crossover exists between these groups). And *Kipplinger's Personal Finance* magazine's 1998 annual forecast issue of upcoming trends highlighted employee napping (or "falling down on the job," as it was humorously described) as a temporary refresher when employees must put in long hours at the office. Among the early converts on this new, more relaxed attitude toward workplace napping were Nike and *MacWorld* magazine.

A nap as short as ten minutes confers proven benefits without lessening your chances for falling asleep that night. According to James B. Maas, author of *Power Sleep*, naps can "quickly restore alertness, enhance performance, reduce mistakes and accidents, and affect profits." Most important, a short nap in the afternoon will restore the mental energy that enables your brain to perform at its best.

When to take the nap? You can either heed the solid Zen principle of sleeping when you feel tired, or you might want to follow the more scientific guidelines suggested by Liz Seymour, who is writing a book on naps. The key, according to Seymour, is to nap within your own personal "zone": the point in the afternoon when your body temperature begins to rise. To determine your zone, calculate the midpoint of your nighttime sleep and add twelve hours. If you go to bed at eleven and get up at seven, your midpoint would be 3:00 A.M. The hour and a half to either side of that time (1:30 to 4:30, in this example) comprises your nap zone for the next afternoon, the period when your brain will maximally benefit from a short nap.

Some sleep experts believe it's not even necessary to fall asleep in order to get some restorative benefits. The worst attitude you can take is to lie down on the sofa in your office with the firm resolution that "I must fall asleep." Instead, simply darken the room, arrange to be called only in the case of true emergencies, and lie quietly with your attention focused on your breathing. Perform the abdominal breathing exercises mentioned earlier. Some people like to concentrate on a sound in the environment, such as the monotonous drone of the air-conditioning unit or the background noise provided by a "white noise" generator kept in their office for the purpose of inducing relaxation. From my experience, you don't need any special equipment and the less formalized the procedure, the better. The idea is to "power down" for twenty to thirty minutes. If you fall asleep during that period, all the better; if you don't, you'll still benefit from the lowered blood pressure, muscle relaxation, temporary freedom from hassle, and, most important, mental rejuvenation.

If you implement the breathing exercises, mental reframing, and timely naps, you will be able to keep mental stress to a minimum, help your brain function at its best, and avoid the loss of neurons in the hippocampus responsible for memory disorders and other brain performance deficits.

27

Use technology to augment your brain's functioning.

*A*t the heart of modern technology is the microchip. No invention in human history has exerted such a profound impact. Today there are nearly 15 billion microchips of some kind in use—the equivalent of two powerful computers for every person in the world. What's more, we haven't even begun to realize the full implications of the microprocessor on our lives.

Thanks to the development of mobile electronic devices— now reduced to dimensions no bigger than a small book—we are no longer tethered to desks and offices, but can work and remain productive almost anywhere. While sitting in a vacation cabin in Maine, we have only to slip a CD into our laptop and we have at our service the *Oxford English Dictionary*. When we couple such resources with the World Wide Web and e-mail, we come up with an information base beyond the dreams of all but the most farseeing technologic prophets a decade ago.

Though experience has always been the driving force for brain development, the nature of that experience has changed over the past several hundred years. Culture rather than biology is now the preeminent influence on brain development (the brain's physical appearance hasn't appreciably changed over the past hundred thousand years). And today, for us, culture is inseparable from brain-power-boosting technology. So, think of your brain as a work in progress that barring injuries or disease is capable of modification over your entire life span. And think of technology not as a threat but as a brain booster. Laptops, for instance, extend the brain's powers and, if used on a consistent basis, become part of that brain.

Philosopher Andy Clark suggests in his book *Being There: Putting Brain, Body, and World Together Again* that "the battery of external props and aids—laptops, filofaxes, texts, maps . . . offset cognitive limitations built into the biological system [of the brain]." These external props are so important that Clark considers the theft of an author's computer as "a very special" kind of crime. Minus the laptop the writer may suffer grievous harm to his creative abilities. "Certain aspects of the external world may be so integral to our cognitive routines as to count *as part of the cognitive machinery* itself."

In short, consider technological aids as coextensions of your brain, capable of enhancing your brain's performance. When you learned to read and write, books, pencils, erasers, and notepads functioned as extensions of your brain. (Of course such extensions depended upon earlier developments: the creation of handwritten scrolls, and books preceded the invention of the printing press.)

More recently, the power of the brain has increased thanks to word processors and other innovations made possible by the advent of the computer chip. By incorporating these aids into your everyday life, you can extend your brain's function in ways not even imaginable only a few years ago.

Andy Clark refers to the new technological extensions of the brain as "wideware" and considers "the relation between the biological organism and the wideware as important and intimate as that of the spider and the web."

Examples of this "wideware" include innovative software programs that can help you enhance different aspects of your brain's performance such as speed of response, working memory, imaging ability, reasoning, calculation, abstraction, and mental endurance.

Far more is involved here than simply the computer leading to an increase in the amount of readily available information. The computer—particularly the laptop computer—is changing the structure and functioning of our brains. Indeed, start thinking of your laptop as an extension of your brain. If this strikes you as a rather odd concept, consider the following points.

What do you do when you want to remember something? First, you make a conscious effort to hold the information in short-term memory and trust that this will result in long-term incorporation. If the information is too complicated or lengthy, you write it down. If there isn't time or opportunity for that, you can dictate the information into a handheld tape recorder for later transcription and editing. In these instances, the pen and the paper and the tape recorder and the transcriber are brain aids: they are functioning as extensions of the brain. But if you're carrying a laptop, you have a one-stop source for your writing and editing. Think of the laptop as a more powerful and refined electronic extension of earlier brain aids like paper and pencil.

With the multigigabyte drive now routinely available on today's laptops, you can cross-correlate today's entries with everything you'll write over the remainder of your life. The laptop makes it possible for you to carry around with you a record of the lifetime productions of your own brain. Within seconds, you can access any personal and professional information that you entered at any earlier point during your life. For instance, I always carry with me a laptop containing the fifteen books I've written, along with my published magazine articles and book reviews. This enables me to compare and contrast what I wrote years ago with what I'm writing now. In the process, thoughts and images of a decade ago influence my present project. Prior to the technology of the printing press, such an experience would have required the memorization of handwritten versions.

Later, after Johannes Gutenberg, such instantaneous access to one's earlier works involved lugging the books around or remaining permanently tethered to a library. The development of the laptop changed all of this.

If you want to get the maximum brain benefit from a laptop, select one that is small, lightweight, and portable enough to carry with you on a fairly constant basis. That doesn't mean dragging it to dinner parties or other social functions, but just having it generally available to record anything and everything related to your private and professional life. On those occasions when a laptop would be awkward or conspicuous, I find it useful to carry a handheld electronic device with me. Later, the palmtop entries can be downloaded onto the laptop. (Incidentally, since you will be entering private and confidential material, password-protect your files no matter what computer you may be using.)

Develop your own files according to your needs. My method is as follows: One entry, simply labeled Journal, is a running narrative of day-to-day events along with my impressions. When making entries, I don't censor or edit my impressions (hence the wisdom of password protection). And I always make certain everything is clearly dated.

In another file labeled Queries, I write down the things that nag me: questions, puzzles, those challenging situations that seem to defy solutions. I print out this material periodically and carry copies with me so that at odd moments I can ponder it. Then I put the printout away and forget about it. I let the solutions percolate in my subconscious and in my dreams.

As situations resolve and my questions are answered, I strike them from the Queries file and enter the solutions into the Journal file. Those questions that remain can best be managed by extracting the main idea, and visually developing it in the form of an association map like the mind map described in chapter 10. This can be done on paper or by using a computer program like Inspiration. A computer-based mind map provides the added advantage of allowing you to incorporate your results into your laptop for integration with the Journal and other files.

The laptop provides not only quicker, easier information access; it also brings about a fundamental change in your subjective experience. By linking your past and present thoughts, insights, and intuitions with your current mental processing, you can achieve a personal synthesis and integration. As discussed in chapter 8, few of us can consciously recall—much less reexperience—our earlier selves. But the laptop makes that possible at any time of our choosing.

Want to revisit the ideas you expressed months or even years ago in a proposal or a term paper or a doctoral dissertation? No problem. Simply bring the document onto the screen. While reading it, the "you" sitting before the screen will be able to revisit the "you" of that earlier time.

Is something happening now that's strongly affecting you? A romantic breakup, a forced job change, a challenging opportunity? Whatever the situation, rapidly enter into the Journal file your thoughts and feelings. Don't censor, don't inhibit, and don't pretend—just put into words as faithfully and accurately as possible what you're thinking and feeling. Weeks or months later when the situation has resolved (hopefully to your satisfaction), your entry will not only jog your memory about details, but you'll *relive* the experience. You'll gain both perspective and insight by comparing your feelings at the moment to your feelings on that earlier occasion.

But before definitely deciding on an electronic journal, consider some of the advantages of a written journal. Having written the first five of my fifteen books by hand and the remainder using a computer, I can well understand the claim that writing things down by hand can exert a powerful effect on your brain's performance. According to Henriette Anne Klauser, author of *Write It Down, Make It Happen,* all of us should carry pen and paper everywhere since "you never know when inspiration will hit." She suggests that writing things down helps the brain retain information because the brain is utilizing a second input channel. While the same thing is true when entering the information in the computer, the process is less intimate and familiar. Only while writing by hand do you actually see your brain's expression in the intimate form of your own handwriting.

While written journals offer unique opportunities for self-expression and exploration, they suffer from several important shortcomings. First, if you want complete access to all of your handwritten productions, you'll eventually be forced to carry several volumes around with you.

Second, written journals are difficult to index. If you suspect a pattern linking your present situation with earlier feelings and thoughts, you may have to spend considerable time paging through your earlier journals searching for those links. With the laptop, you have only to enter a few words or phrases and you can locate and correlate entries separated by many years. (You also don't have to deal with the handwriting problem—which, if you're like me, can be formidable. Handwriting, like other physical characteristics, changes over the years; that entry set down with passion and conviction several years ago may later turn out to be unreadable.)

Third, computer searches via your laptop frequently turn up surprise connections you would not have considered searching for. You might discover, for instance, that your use of a certain word or phrase to describe someone serves as a prediction of interpersonal troubles ahead. Tacit knowledge—knowing more than we can find words to explain or are even aware of—is often uncovered via use of the search function of electronic journals.

Finally, you can easily modify computer journals—adding attachments, incorporating the results of web searches, and consulting CD-based encyclopedias or dictionaries like my favorite, *The New Shorter Oxford English Dictionary*.

But more important than any of these uses, the electronic journal offers you the opportunity for self-analysis and self-commentary. I often return to earlier entries and add new material, usually in italics, or in a different font, in order to show that the entries occurred at a different time. Sometimes I add simple comments to the earlier entry; on other occasions I take the role of the omniscient author (for example, "Little did I know that within a week of writing that critical comment about Robert, he would be diagnosed with the leukemia that would eventually kill him").

To assist you in the creation of an electronic journal, I'd suggest you use one of the extremely small voice recorders with a built-in flash memory. Mine weighs only 2.3 ounces and fits in the palm of my hand. By a simple press of the Record button, I can capture fleeting thoughts, observations, and impressions. On those occasions when I hear something interesting or find myself engaged in a stimulating conversation, I record it. At a later point, I can transfer what I want of this material to my journal.

Several of the flash memory recorders have the capability for direct downloading to your PC. With an investment of some time and effort, the recording can be directly transcribed into text via a voice recognition system. Finally, the flash memory recorder can be used as a memory aid. Before leaving home for work, for instance, dictate into the recorder all of the things you want to accomplish and then listen to the list at the end of the day when you can't remember any more items. You will no doubt come up with some original ways of incorporating the flash memory recorder and your electronic journal.

Of course, you can write both by hand and with a word processor. Novelist Umberto Eco varies the two methods when working on his books. "People always think that either you do or you do not work on a computer," Eco mentioned in a 1989 interview. "False. There are pages and pages that are handwritten along with many other pages that are written on the computer." So if you decide to use both a handwritten and an electronic journal, you're in good company.

When working on your computer journal, you might also want to combine your efforts with some creative and exploratory web surfing. Sherry Terkle of MIT says that "computers are objects to think with" and suggests we consider the laptop not just as a technical instrument but as "the subjective computer."

Terkle adds, "While online, you aren't just a unitary ego but something more fluid, a kind of decentered identity." She recommends that we use our computers as a means for self-exploration. Try using your computer to write short stories in which you can involve changes in gender, interests, or activity patterns: if you're a married male lawyer, you might pretend to be a twentysomething female biker. What changes do you experience while role-playing in this way and with this new and totally unfamiliar identity?

Your goal is to achieve insight into your cognitive and emotional processing. This knowledge will not only provide enlightenment; through variation, change, and novelty it will also free up your mental energies, an important first step toward making your brain work more efficiently.

28

Concentrate on and act in harmony with your natural abilities.

It's important to take into account how your learning as an adult differs from how you learned earlier in your life. First and foremost, *adult learning is self-directed*. By adulthood, we generally know our strengths and weaknesses. As a result of this self-knowledge, most of us enter careers in which we can best apply our natural talents and thereby increase our chances for success. But this opportunity for self-selection isn't always available until late in our education. Not until the final years of college can we pick courses that we want to take instead of courses we have to take in order to fulfill degree requirements. This delay before students can plot their own course of study partly explains those late bloomers who, free for the first time in their lives to choose their own educational directions through self-directed learning, often achieve greater success than any of their teachers ever predicted. They do this by playing to their strengths. You should do this, too, by concentrating on your natural abilities.

Take the advice of Peter Drucker, author of *The Effective Executive*:

> For years I have urged managers to concentrate their efforts in areas in which they are strong and to waste as little effort as possible trying to improve the areas in which they don't have much confidence.... You may be shocked when you identify your weaknesses in certain skills or your lack of talent for certain activities. Use the information to avoid jobs that depend on those skills rather than waste time challenging yourself.

Drucker's advice, of course, runs counter to traditional wisdom that encourages us to put greater effort into overcoming our weaknesses. But traditional wisdom ignores the fact that each person's brain operates most efficiently when it's involved in activities it does best. And those activities will differ from one person to another. Each person's brain is unique, and this distinctiveness explains why people are drawn to particular careers.

So, in regard to your career, follow your strengths. But when it comes to aspects of your life other than your career, give some credence to the advice of Mark Twain: "Make it a point to do something every day that you don't want to do." The basis for this masochistic-sounding advice? Simply put, the brain is both marvelously adaptive and at the same time more than a little lazy. This is particularly true when it comes to intellectual activity.

"Everyone is ignorant, only on different subjects," as Eleanor Roosevelt put it. Unfortunately, the human brain has a natural tendency to deal with those subjects it's best suited for to the exclusion of everything else.

Let's hypothesize, for instance, that Jones, a wealthy banker, hates the opera. But his wife, Lisa, a publicist for the Metropolitan Opera, drags him to the opening night of *The Magic Flute*. At the postperformance party, Jones's wife introduces him to the internationally famous tenor Manicotti, and the two men are left to talk alone. Both men are tired, and after five minutes of stilted conversation, bordering on antagonism, they are ready to make their excuses and part company. Talk of New York Stock Exchange fluctuations now, compared to last year, is of no interest to Manicotti, who lives on a farm in Italy most of the year, and the irritating fact that the stand-in soprano didn't reach her high notes in the "Queen of the Night" aria falls on Jones's deaf ears. Clearly, the experience in differing neuronal networks that distinguished each of these men's brains has left little room for a "meeting of the minds." Unfortunately for all of us, the brain has a natural tendency to deal with those subjects it is best suited for, to the exclusion and intolerance of all else. But it is a mistake to impose the limited pattern of our specialized knowledge (career) on the world beyond. Both Jones and Manicotti realize this when they witness Lisa's furious glance in their direction, so they hurriedly adjust their mental goalposts in an effort to seek out common ground. After renewed effort, they later discover a shared passion for wines. An hour later, Lisa must forcibly extract her husband from the discussion of "white versus red" in order to go home. She drives.

If you were never good at languages, sign up for a language course. Or try teaching yourself a foreign language by means of tapes that you can play in the car on the way to work. It is important to achieve a balance: art, music, business, manual skills, and the sciences. If your education and training is in the humanities, then force yourself to learn about quantum mechanics or, even better, the brain. In any bookstore or library you can find excellent science books written for readers with little previous interest in science (I have written twelve books on the human brain that fit into that category). If your education and career involve science, then force yourself in your spare time to learn about opera, ballet, or classical literature.

Whatever your background, indulge your natural curiosity. Only the adult learner has that privilege. This is especially important if, as I suggested, you follow Drucker's advice about playing to your strengths in your work life. If you follow his advice about careers (and you should), it's vitally important that you make every effort to avoid becoming unbalanced and overspecialized in your private life.

Keep in mind the key ingredients to successful adult learning:

- A sense of challenge
- An optimum state of arousal: not anxious, but alert and vigilant
- A free-floating attention so that links can be made
- Some form of feedback process, such as learning along with others, or, if learning alone, creating tape-recorded summaries of new information as it's learned

In practical terms, look for ways of sharing your new knowledge with others. When knowledge is shared, everybody grows and evolves. This doesn't do away with individual expression and accomplishment, but it does make life and learning more interesting and playful.

●●●

At this point, you have twenty-eight suggestions to help you get the best performance from your brain. Read them over frequently and look for ways of applying them. Since getting smart and staying smart involves learning as much as possible about your brain, start off by reading any of the popular books on the brain listed in "Resources." And get started on your electronic journal. The written expression of your day-to-day thoughts and experiences will serve as your anchoring point. If you're completely honest and spontaneous in your entries, you'll achieve useful insights into your personality and your brain's functioning. And since wide reading plays such an important role in getting and staying smart, begin making entries in your reading journal.

Keep reminding yourself that as the result of millions of years of evolution, the human brain is capable of directing its own future development. As the Dalai Lama put it in a lecture he gave on the Mall in Washington, D.C., "What distinguishes us human beings from other forms of life is that we have far more powerful mental experiences in the forms of thoughts and emotions." We have our brains to thank for that distinction, which separates us from the rest of the animal world.

But getting smart and staying smart doesn't just happen: You have to work at it. And as I hope I have convinced you by now, training your brain and learning more about its functioning is the most powerful way of making you smarter. Not only will you learn a lot about yourself and how to increase your mental efficiency, you'll also have a lot of fun in the process.

Resources

BOOKS

David L. Book, *Problems for Puzzlebusters* (Washington, D.C.: Enigmatics Press, 1992).

Ian Glynn, *An Anatomy of Thought* (New York: Oxford, 1999).

Gary Klein, *Sources of Power: How People Make Decisions* (Cambridge, Mass.: MIT Press, 1998).

Carol Krucoff and Mitchell Krucoff, *Healing Moves: How to Cure, Relieve and Prevent Common Ailments with Exercise* (New York: Harmony Books, 2000).

Richard Leviton, *Brain Builders: A Lifelong Guide to Sharper Thinking, Better Memory, and an Age-Proof Mind* (Upper Saddle River, N.J.: Prentice Hall, 1995).

Harry Lorrayne and Jerry Lucas, *The Memory Book* (Lanham, Mass.: Barnes & Noble Books, 1993).

Vervon Mark, M.D., with Jeffrey P. Mark, *Brain Power: A Neurosurgeon's Complete Program to Maintain and Enhance Brain Fitness throughout Your Life* (Boston: Houghton Mifflin, 1989).

Eric McLuhan, *Electric Language: Understanding the Message* (New York: Buzz Books, 1998).

Snowdon Parlette, *The Brain Workout: Aerobics for the Mind* (New York: M. Evans, 1997).

Richard Restak, *Brainscapes* (New York: Hyperion, 1995).

Richard Restak, *The Modular Brain* (New York: Charles Scribner's Sons, 1994).

Richard Restak, *Mysteries of the Mind* (Washington, D.C.: National Geographic, 2000).

Daniel L. Schacter, *The Seven Sins of Memory* (Boston: Houghton Mifflin, 2001).

Daniel M. Wegner, *White Bears and Other Unwanted Thoughts: Suppression, Obsession, and the Psychology of Mental Control* (New York: Viking, 1989).

GAMES

Levinger Crossword Dice (Delray Beach, Fla.: Levinger).

Nob Yoshigahara, Rush Hour Traffic Jam Puzzle (Alexandria, Va.: Binary Arts).

Marsha J. Falco, Set: The Family Game of Visual Perception (Ravensburg, Germany: Ravensburger).

Tangoes: The Ancient Chinese Puzzle Game (San Francisco: Rex Games).

Visual Brainstorm (Alexandria, Va.: Binary Arts).

COMPUTER PROGRAMS
Inspiration: The Visual Thinking Tool (Portland, Oreg.: Inspiration Software, Inc.).

WORKBOOK PROGRAMS
Robert Allen, Philip Carter, and Ken Russell, *Mensa Mind Games: Over 200 Puzzles, Games and Exercises to Maximize Your Brainpower* (London: Carlton Books, 1997).

Andi Bell, *The Memory Pack: Everything You Need to Supercharge Your Memory and Master Your Life* (London: Carlton Books, 2000).

Jonathan Hancock, *Memory Power: Memory-Building Skills for Everyday Situations* (Hauppauge, N.Y.: Barrons, 1997).

WEBSITES
Since websites come and go, let me suggest two current favorites and, more important, an approach to obtaining the most current sites. Start with a favorite search engine (Altavista is my personal favorite) and enter "brainteasers." This will bring up my personal favorites, *http://www.puzz.com* and *http://www.puzzles.com,* which features a cornucopia of challenges. After mining that source (including suggested links), enter "puzzles" as the search term and you'll discover my second favorite, *http://www.thinks.com,* which includes a host of different puzzles, including some unusual ones such as puzzles by Lewis Carroll or puzzles challenging your knowledge of original illustrations and quotes from the works of Charles Dickens. Since learning and brain improvement should be fun, try out the humor site *http://www.dilbert.com.* Check out the daily mental workout in order to "avoid the cerebral stagnation brought about by mindless meetings, endless e-mail, and re-writing reports for the boss." And for the humorous part of Dilbert, check out the puzzles designed for your boss's brain. Remember: If one site closes, another one opens, so try your favorite search engine and enter words like "brainteaser," "puzzle," "anagram," "logical challenges," and so on. Use your own imagination in order to come up with terms that will yield both language-based puzzles, such as various versions of the daily crossword (varying in difficulty), to challenges directed to the nonverbal, pictorial powers of your right hemisphere.

Richard Restak, M.D., a practicing neurologist and neuropsychiatrist, is a clinical professor of neurology at George Washington University School of Medicine and Health Sciences. Born in Wilmington, Delaware, Dr. Restak went on to receive his medical degree from Georgetown University School of Medicine. He is the author of twelve previous books on the brain, including the best-selling *The Brain*, as well as *The Mind* and *The Brain Has a Mind of Its Own*. Dr. Restak's publications have appeared in *The New York Times Book Review*, the *Washington Post*, *Smithsonian Magazine*, and *Sciences*. He is a consultant for *National Geographic* magazine and an occasional commentator for National Public Radio's *Morning Edition*, and he lectures widely on topics about mental performance and developments in brain research. Dr. Restak has three adult daughters and lives with his wife in Washington, D.C.